Praise for *Rookie Mistakes*

"*Rookie Mistakes* is a hilarious and thoughtfully written guide to becoming a real-life grown up. I nodded along, often laughing, while reading the relatable stories of Kelly's life that so many of us can identify with."

KATIE CRENSHAW, BESTSELLING AUTHOR OF *HER BODY CAN*

"It can be all too easy to look back on our rookie mistakes with nothing but regret and embarrassment. Instead, Kelly invites us to consider our younger selves with kindness, and of course, good humor. Readers will enjoy her stories, laugh aloud, and leave with a little more grace for the time it takes us all to learn through experience."

MEREDITH MILLER, PASTOR AND HOST OF THE *ASK AWAY PODCAST*

"With unflinching honesty and peak relatability, Bandas delivers the book we need right now. Dripping with 90's aesthetic, *Rookie Mistakes* cracked me up, made me think, and reminded me that I'm not alone in this disorienting world. Spoiler alert: *Rookie Mistakes* is a sneaky, cackle-worthy guide to being human. Read it and find yourself somehow more alive."

SHANNAN MARTIN, AUTHOR OF *THE MINISTRY OF ORDINARY PLACES* AND *FALLING FREE*

"Honestly, who gave Kelly Bandas the right? Who gave her the right to be hilarious, hot, and a gifted writer? Kelly serves in the space where it's not the end of the world to mess up, and bonus: she got a good story out of it. Enjoy this book like you would a night out with some of your oldest and dearest—shutting down the restaurant, belly full of good food, scream-singing Semisonic's "Closing Time" at the top of your lungs."

Erin Moon, cohost of *The Bible Binge Podcast*

"Kelly takes us down the back roads of our childhood. Softly swaying with the windows rolled down. I can feel the wind on my face and the force of the breeze as I fly my arm plane out the window. She takes us to that time where our innocence is rife. Where we first heard that we were not enough. As we are. Where we first learned the beauty of the mundane. Even if only years later. This book is brimming with Kodak moments that you see and feel at once. It's an immersive experience. She takes you to the familiar. Maybe, even, the long forgotten. She sifts through the non-adjudicated moments of our past and finds the gold. And points us to it. Kelly's voice is so funny and fresh, she'll have you laughing out loud. By yourself. In your bed. She is a generous journeyman and guide. You will be so glad you took this tour with her. You'll come out on the other side, remembering your past differently and enjoying more of the moments that made you, you. In a world that is overcome with uncertainty and jagged edges, this was the consistent soft spot I visited daily. Her humor is wide and deep. But so is her wisdom."

Cha Barefield, host of *The Cha Show*

Rookie Mistakes

Rookie Mistakes

a grown-up's field guide to getting your act together

Kelly Bandas

W Publishing Group
An Imprint of Thomas Nelson

Rookie Mistakes

Published in Nashville, Tennessee, by W Publishing, an imprint of Thomas Nelson.

Thomas Nelson titles may be purchased in bulk for educational, business, fundraising, or sales promotional use. For information, please email SpecialMarkets@ThomasNelson.com.

ISBN 978-0-7852-8841-1 (audiobook)
ISBN 978-0-7852-8840-4 (eBook)
ISBN 978-0-7852-8831-2 (TP)

Library of Congress Cataloging-in-Publication Data

Library of Congress Control Number: 2021950479

Printed in the United States of America

22 23 24 25 26 LSC 10 9 8 7 6 5 4 3 2 1

To the Bandas Boys.

Contents

Part 4: The Realizing-That-Getting-Your-Act-Together-Takes-Your-Whole-Life Part: "Hey, Alexa, Order More Toilet Paper"

Introduction

As a person who has spent most of her life skipping pages numbered by Roman numerals, I would like to take a moment to applaud you for choosing to read this introduction. Especially because no one will ever know if you flip forward a few pages and reallocate the time you just saved to another equally important task, like

a. picking at your cuticles;
b. walking to the other side of your house to get that—crap, what did I come over here for?; or
c. eating an apple for a snack and then LOL-ing two minutes later when you get back up to get Extra Toasty Cheez-Its or whatever your preferred *real* snack might be.

But now that you've identified yourself as the type of person who reads the Roman-numeral pages, I would also like to preemptively apologize for the inevitable moment when your partner or child or roommate interrupts your reading time to ask you where you are in your book and you have to do rapid-fire mental math to decipher what *lv* means. (Just kidding, I would *never* ask you to read a fifty-plus-page introduction, but I needed to make it a hard Roman numeral and not something like *iii.*)

So good job, and also, I'm sorry.

You know, now that I think about it, this "Good job/I'm sorry" vibe is exactly how most of my real-life introductions seem to shake out. Although they usually start something like this:

ME: "Hi, New Friend!"
NEW FRIEND: "Hey!"
ME: "I love your sweater."
NEW FRIEND: "Thank you! I love *your* sweater!"
ME: "This old thing? I literally paid 75 cents for this at a dog's garage sale."
NEW FRIEND: "I love animals!"

You know the drill: You meet a new person, say something nice about her outfit and something self-deprecating about your own, begin sharing random pieces of personal trivia and quicker than you can say, "Oh my gosh, I *also* love podcasts," you are bored of the small talk and ready to get into the good stuff. You know, the stuff that isn't just about your new friend's work or most recent vacation or favorite show on Netflix (even if it's *Outlander*—but *maybe* if it's *Outlander* because . . . I'M REALLY INTO THAT SHOW RIGHT NOW, OKAY?!).

The good stuff is the real stuff—the stuff that connects us and makes each of us grow. And for me, listening to the good stuff typically generates one of two responses:

1) "Good job."
or
2) "I'm sorry."

Maybe I'm oversimplifying things here, but it seems to me that our relationships with other human beings could be much better served if we all said those two phrases a lot more. Not because they fix anything or absolve us of the responsibility of taking action and growing ourselves, but because they make whomever we are talking to know they are seen, valued, and important. Whether you're offering an "I'm sorry" because of a stressful family situation or a "Good job" because your new friend finally figured out how to sync her iCal with her Google calendar, it doesn't matter. What does matter is that we use our time together as a means of investing in our relationship, helping each other feel seen, and hopefully having some laughs while we do it.

One thing you should know about me before we get started is that I've always been a bit of a perfectionist. Someone who derived a hearty chunk of her self-worth from doing things the "right" way: having each of my three kids on the perfect nap schedule, making sure I never drove a mile past what the

Valvoline sticker on my windshield dictated, and so on. And don't get me wrong, those things were okay because that's who I am as a person—and maybe it's how you are too. I think a lot of us need that kind of control in our own lives when the outside world feels . . . let's call it *out of whack*.

But what I began discovering as my need for being right and in control started to make each day feel more like a to-do list and less of a life, was that maybe I was prioritizing rightness over connection. I could blame it on being an Enneagram One, but I prefer to call it by another name: *a rookie mistake*—something I thought I was doing right, until I realized I wasn't. We've all been there—so sure of ourselves in one situation or another, until something or someone comes along to change our perspective. It's kind of like when we all thought low-rise jeans were a good look, until someone introduced us to the high-rise.

But this time, instead of denim, it's our behavior.

I have to be transparent and admit to you all that when I first started writing this book, I truly believed the majority of my rookie mistakes were going to be nicely relegated to the adolescent-heavy chapters and my adult life would be full of little nuggets of wisdom to share. However, it turns out that, no matter how old I get, I have yet to become impervious to mistake-making—which is great for content, but less great for all those wisdom nuggets I was hoping for.

What became clear through this writing process was that I'm pretty sure there are more people out there who feel the same way. And maybe we're missing an opportunity to learn from each other because we're all so busy hiding our mistakes for fear of looking foolish, when sharing them with each other might actually draw us closer together and give us the opportunity to show courage through change.

Throughout this book, you'll watch me make more cringey mistakes than Edith from *Downton Abbey,* but I firmly believe it's through sharing our screw-ups and changes of heart that we can forge true connections and grow throughout the course of our lives.

So let's get into the good stuff together, shall we? Although, admittedly, I'm about to do most of the talking, feel free to interject whenever you see fit. Respond in the margins, send me an email, or just talk right into the pages like I do when I'm role-playing with my shampoo bottles in the shower, practicing for a podcast interview that's never going to happen (*cough* *Conan O'Brien* *cough*). Bonus points if after reading this you're inspired to share your rookie mistakes with me or your friends in real life. (But also please tell me too. I don't want to feel left out.)

However you spend your time during the next 200-something pages, I'm really glad you're here. And also—cute sweater.

Part 1

The Kid Part

Dying of a Guilty Conscience and Other Totally Normal Childhood Fears

CHAPTER 1

Size 6X

I was a chubby kid for the better part of my childhood. In the early nineties, polite people might have called me "sturdy." Regular people would've just called me fat. I have very clear memories of searching for a size 6X dress for First Communion and "husky" jeans in the Lord & Taylor youth section, and outright refusing to wear pants that fastened with a button until the third grade. Why pants makers decided to put the pinchiest part of the pants right at my squishiest spot, I'll never understand.

At birth, however, I was runway-model skinny, weighing in at just under seven pounds. What a babe-y! I could fit into literally any onesie in my closet without even sucking in, and my mom had to use the tightest Velcro position on my Pampers.[1] But living on an all-liquid diet didn't suit me for long, and before you could say "pureed prunes," I had rubber-band baby wrists and a trifecta of chins, like a teensy-weensy Chris Farley, living in a Pack 'n Play down by the river.

Now from the outside looking in, being a fat kid isn't a big deal, or rather, it shouldn't be a big deal. And it's not. Not at all. Until suddenly it is. And then it's a very big deal.

Yet despite what TV and society and kids at school thought about my appearance, my childhood was a blissful time during which I didn't bat an eye at the idea of eating three bagels with butter in one sitting or consistently saying yes to the waffle cone upgrade option at my beloved Steve's Ice Cream in Lexington Center, which was conveniently located just steps away from my favorite Italian restaurant. If I wanted it, I ate it. And I wanted it all—with sprinkles. Now this is where you might be thinking, *Where were her parents during this torrid eating-fest she called a childhood?* And you'd be right to think that. Because so far, I haven't mentioned them. So this is the part of the story when I tell you I emancipated myself as a toddler.

No, no, that's not true—and I don't want to start off this relationship by lying to you. But the honest answer is that my parents never mentioned anything at all about my weight or my tendency to supersize whenever possible.[2] I think they

1. This might've been a little bit about some hip dysplasia I was dealing with, but for our purposes here, let's just pretend it's because I was a baby Kate Moss.
2. A very big deal and incredibly progressive for nineties parents, so yay Mom and Dad!

never mentioned it because I was basically a sweet kid. And a smart kid. And a relatively nice kid. So no one really cared that there was a little extra of me to love. In fact, my mom says she doesn't even remember me "being all that chubby."

And my weight didn't really bother me either. I found joy in eating two bowls of cereal after school while I watched reruns of *I Love Lucy,* so I ate them while shouting, "What's for dinner?" to my mom between mouthfuls. I drank regular Coke and always upgraded to the large value-meal option with extra dipping sauce when our family hit the Burger King drive-thru. I sat in the front seat of our family's minivan[3] (as was my birthright as oldest child), and my three younger siblings would shout their orders to me so I could relay them to Mom in one of the most calorie-dense versions of the game Telephone ever played.

If we're going for historical accuracy, I would order six packets of dipping sauce—either BBQ or honey mustard, depending on the season. Honey mustard was clearly a cooler weather sauce, while BBQ was reserved for the warm summer months when we ate our fast food in the driveway and attempted to lure ants to their deaths by squishing them on leftover french fries. Of course, this was during the glory days of fast food, long before they started charging customers for the sauces that made their food edible in the first place. Just who do these fast-food executives think is out there eating

3. A Chrysler Town and Country, to be exact, which is of no consequence except that it's the exact same make and model of the minivan I currently take Spotify music requests from my kids in.

their salty-ass fries dry? What kind of shriveled-up, uncivilized troll would enjoy that? Not me. I had a refined palate.

It was during one particular outdoor luncheon feast when I was about seven (I remember that it was summer, because I was dipping fries in BBQ sauce) that a neighbor kid named Kevin bluntly asked why I needed so many sauce packets for my food. His question was most likely brought on because I had repeatedly asked our group of neighborhood friends if they were going to finish their fries, and if not, could I have them.

"Haven't you had enough fries already? Plus, you're like—so chubby."

Who me?

The girl who wears T-shirts from her dad's closet and youth XL bicycle shorts? The one who licks her finger to wipe her plate clean, especially when eating a cheese-based meal? *Me?*

Surely this neighbor kid was just trying to assert some kind of veiled toxic masculinity and make a totally bogus comment before running back over to his house to grab his dumb bike that didn't *even have gears.* He didn't really think I was fat. And besides, I didn't feel chubby. I felt normal. I felt like a normal kid who was eating her dream lunch before she scurried off to ride her bike around the neighborhood, with some BBQ sauce in the corners of her mouth (for later).

But as I peeled out of my driveway after lunch on my awesome bike (*with gears, Kevin*) the sting of the word *fat* pounded in my ears. Because being fat was bad; I knew that. And if I was fat and fat was bad, then, by the transitive property, I, Kelly, the little girl who just learned how to ride her bike with no hands for almost four full pedals, was also bad. So bad, that I would feel the need to spend the next few decades punishing my body out of fear that some other *Kevin* out there also wouldn't like the way I looked, which is, honestly, a degree of power I don't believe should be entrusted to any Kevin—ever. And I'm not talking about your one Uncle Kev who's a total treasure; I'm talking about the theoretical Kevins who pass out eating disorders and self-doubt by making snarky comments or selling only straight-size clothing in their stores. Their powers should be revoked.

But seven-year-old me didn't get any of that yet. It would be three full years before comments like that would lead to my first calorie-restricting diet. Gee whiz! I had so much innocence left to enjoy! So for the time being, I shoved those burgeoning feelings of inadequacy aside so I could focus on much more important things, like getting to *five* full pedals with no hands.

CHAPTER 2

OshKosh M'gosh

When I was seven, I had this pair of really slick OshKosh B'gosh overalls that I wore all the time. They were a classic denim wash, with a little pocket in the front where you could tuck literally anything you might need during the day: Mike and Ikes, Starbursts, Skittles. I myself used it exclusively for sugary snacks, but that was my journey. Incidentally, these overalls also had a pair of buttons by the waist on each side that I could use to create a little more "digestion space" after eating all my delicious pocket candy. It was kind of like when adults unbutton a top button on their Dockers after a big Thanksgiving meal—except it was for small, fat kids, and it was glorious.

I liked these overalls not just for their candy-holding ability, but also because of their versatility: both straps on, straps crisscrossed in the back, one strap hanging down so it could dip in the toilet when I peed—and because they provided a little counterpressure on my protruding belly. Kind of like a weighted blanket, with straps and pockets.

There is ample photographic evidence of me in these overalls and, in most of the pictures, I'm usually sporting a smart, ear-pinchy headband or glittery slap bracelet to complete the ensemble. It was my most nineties look, and I would honestly pay $500 to be able to recreate it exactly today—right down to the overly thick, bright pink laces in my high-tops that we bought from Bob's (my family's favorite *ultra*-New England-y discount clothing store). They were definitely off-brand and had some kind of four-point star that looked more like a nod to a Satanic cult than the Converse logo. But despite my passion for my beloved overalls, I wasn't allowed to wear them every day. My mom had this weird idea that we needed to at least give the illusion they were being washed between wears, so I padded my wardrobe with stirrup leggings and oversize Cape Cod sweatshirts to fill in the gaps between my beloved overalls days.

On one unseasonably warm spring afternoon, I was riding my bike around our neighborhood cul-de-sac in one such oversize Cape Cod garment when I saw my dad's Chevy truck pulling into the driveway much earlier than usual. Handlebar streamers billowing in the wind, I hyperpedaled for the house, anxious to see what would bring him home from work before his usual six o'clock. My mom was coming out of the house at the same time, drying some hand wetness of unknown origin on her clothes and looking slightly exasperated. "He still doesn't want to go," she said in my dad's general direction.

"What do you mean he 'doesn't want to go'? I got these tickets specifically to take *him.*" My dad, usually a stick-with-the-plan type of guy, the kind who put his socks and New Balance sneakers on immediately after showering, was visibly frustrated that his intentions for the evening were apparently being crapped on by the whims of my younger brother, Mark, who he'd planned to surprise with a father-son trip to watch the Red Sox play.

My parents went back and forth like this for a little while, my eyes ping-ponging back and forth between them trying to decode the reason for my dad's upset while remaining totally inconspicuous as I rode in one hundred figure-eights around our driveway. Apparently, in refusing my dad's invitation, my younger brother was passing up an important little boy rite of passage. Even though it was supposed to be a special treat. Even though my dad had cut out of work early for it. And even though the tickets were wicked expensive. Despite being a card-carrying b-o-y, Mark just didn't want to participate in this obligatory male-bonding sesh; he just wanted to stay home, eat some Gushers, and maybe trap a salamander before dinner. Activities which, in my opinion, sounded cool, but not hang-out-by-yourself-with-your-dad cool—just like regular-old-Tuesday-night cool.

Maybe it was my ultrahard, plastic headband cutting off

the blood supply to my brain, but it never occurred to me to ask my dad if I could go in Mark's place. If anything, I figured the rules of the Royal Family would be in play here, thus naming my two-year-old brother Jack next in line for the ticket. And truthfully, I didn't really care about watching the Red Sox play at Fenway Park, especially as the second-choice kid, but I did want to spend time with my dad and maybe get a hot dog with ketchup. When you're in second grade, that's a top-tier evening.

Using everything I'd learned from watching the movie *E.T.* over fifty times, I attempted to telepathically will my brother to remain unmoved by our parents' promises of staying up late *and* cotton candy. And when I finally heard my mom whisper, "Maybe you should just take Kelly," I executed an enthusiastic, silent fist pump, in the most epically nineties way you could imagine.

With the forty-five-minute drive into Boston and traffic and parking to consider—and factoring in the extra ninety minutes my parents always insisted on allotting for any family excursion—there wasn't much time to waste. I hightailed it up to my room and pulled my overalls out of the drawer. This was a special occasion and, as such, concessions could be made regarding exceeding my overalls-wearing quota. I completed my look by throwing on my red Little League baseball cap, the one with the mesh back and giant C on the squishy, foam front. I looked exactly like Ice Box from *Little Giants*, which, if you translate my seven-year-old standards into current-day reality TV–speak, meant I looked as fabulous and empowered as Chrishell from season 2 of *Selling Sunset.*

I rode all the way to Fenway in the front seat of my dad's truck, secured by a lap seatbelt boasting enough slack to fit both me and my invisible conjoined twin. We listened to the *Sports Talk* guys yell about how Red Sox general manager Lou Gorman couldn't expect third baseman Wade Boggs to carry the team on his back and why the Sox could really use a healthy Mike Greenwell in the outfield. And although I couldn't have told you the difference between an ERA and an RBI, I knew enough to nod along in agreement with the boisterous radio chatter, if for no other reason than to assert that I deserved to be a part of the conversation. Every now and then, Dad would chime in, as if he were sitting in the WEEI 850 AM radio booth, too, often making observations seconds before the on-air guys would. He was like some kind of clairvoyant baseball oracle who knew things about the game reserved only for insider professionals.

During the commercial breaks Dad played tour guide, pointing out the trademark features of Boston to me and indoctrinating me into true Bostonian culture: the Harvard campus on both sides of the Charles River, the DeWolfe boathouse, the Fens, the Citgo Sign—a yellow brick road of landmarks all leading to his favorite, under-the-radar gas station parking lot, which didn't promise *not* to block you in, but *did* only cost fifteen dollars. With each kernel of knowledge (or maybe I should say Cracker Jack) my dad shared with me, I started to feel less and less like the second-choice kid. I was only seven, but I'd seen enough Disney Channel original movies to know the boys in the family were supposed to be the ones at the game with Dad. I was supposed to be at home with my mom saying things like, "A little help here?" when the lightbulb in my Easy-Bake Oven burned my sad, single-serving brownie.

But tonight at least, that wasn't the case. Tonight, I was walking down Yawkey Way, holding hands with my dad, scanning the crowd for the best place to buy a souvenir after the game, as a chorus of ticket scalpers filled the night air with their cries of "Who needs two? Anybody got two?" We eked our way toward the entrance, between Italian sausage vendors and fans wearing Red Sox jerseys, Dad squeezing my hand a little tighter as the crowd swelled around us.

"This is us right here," he pointed toward Gate A, both our tickets in his hand. "Here comes the best part!" His excitement was meant for both of us: me seeing the field at Fenway Park for the first time and my dad seeing me see the field at Fenway Park for the first time. Both equally transformative experiences.

After the excitement of getting to the park and finding our seats in the upper grandstand, the game itself proved to be utterly forgettable. I don't even remember who we were playing. There were probably some home runs and stolen bases and, if we were lucky, some tense words between manager Butch Hobson and the home plate umpire. You know, one of those numbers where two men would bump chests and act like they're going to fight until one of the other umpires yells, "You're outta here!" which is essentially the sports version of "I'm telling Mom!"

Even now, as an adult, I always love a good baseball fight, because there really isn't anything better for female empowerment than watching grown men in uniforms with little characters printed on them go at each other. It just sucks the bravado out of the whole thing and turns it into a sporty version of *Newsies*. What, are we not supposed to giggle when the Cardinals fight the Blue Jays? They're *birdies*!

Regardless of what was going on in the game, Dad and I left shortly before the seventh-inning stretch. It was getting late and I'd run out of snacks to ask for, so we drove home listening to the rest of the game on the radio, Dad occasionally punching his fist in the air when the Sox did something good, and me paying close attention to exactly what made him do that. My dad explained the real rules of baseball to me that night. He told me about how he used to go to games when he was a kid and watch future Hall of Famers and about how October 1984 was one of the best and worst months of his life. Without knowing it, he told me all the things he would've told my brother Mark and, in doing that, opened up a way for us to be more than just a dad and his daughter. He offered me a place in his life I had assumed was reserved for just the guys and, in doing so, built a bridge into our future.

There have probably been a hundred more overtly meaningful moments between my dad and me over the years—like the winter night he saved my life after I'd fallen in a deep, dark hole in our backyard, or the moment he held my oldest child (and his first grandchild) in his arms for the very first time. But there was something about that not-so-special night at the Red Sox game that sealed a very important fate for Dad and me. Because after my brother declined his invitation, it would've been all too easy for him to catch the game with a beer-drinking buddy, who more than likely would've made it past the seventh-inning stretch. But instead, my dad took me.

It may not seem like earthshaking stuff, but I've found that most things don't while they're happening. More often than not, it's those seemingly insignificant, not-that-big-of-a-deal moments that end up shaping who we are and who we become. For me, it was the gallant and unnecessary act of my dad taking the time to experience something that he loved with me. I have no doubt that I ended up loving baseball (and my dad) as much as I do because he cared enough to share a simple game with me that night.

There were a lot of photos taken of me in my favorite overalls when I was seven, but my very favorite one turned up a few weeks after that baseball game. I had gone to the mailbox after school and found a printed piece of cardstock lying on top of a pile of bills and magazines. I can't remember what it was advertising, probably a bank or something else equally irrelevant in the world of a seven-year-old, but something about it caught my eye. Right there on the front of that advertisement was a picture of my dad and me, sitting in the grandstand with a crowd of thirty-five thousand at Fenway Park. Just two tiny, blurry bodies watching as some Sox player stood in the batter's box. Dad's arm was around my seatback, and I was staring straight ahead, waiting for whatever was about to happen with the next pitch. I could barely make out our faces, but I knew it was us. A picture of my dad and me, forever immortalized on a piece of junk mail, at my very first Red Sox game.

CHAPTER 3

Guinea Pig Heaven

I murdered a guinea pig once. Which, I get, sounds superbad. You throw the word *murder* around in a sentence and suddenly people start getting all kinds of horrible ideas about what kind of person you are. And I'm sure your mind is racing, because we don't know each other all that well yet and you thought this was going to be a fun book to suggest for book club and suddenly you're freaking out, because if this ends up being superweird, that's on you. Let me take a moment to assuage your fears and assure you that this is not going to be the beginning of a story about how pet-killing acted as a catalyst for a life of crime and/or breeding bizarre, exotic animals for a roadside zoo outside of Tampa. It's chapter about celebrating what you are instead of feeling bad about what you're not.

The first thing you need to know is the honest-to-goodness truth that I didn't mean to leave Belle in her cage for a whole week without food and water. I didn't intentionally set out to murder her in cold blood. It was an accident. *An accident, I tell you!* I still maintain that had the whole issue gone to trial, the jury would've returned with a verdict of involuntary pet slaughter and I most likely wouldn't have done any hard time.

And yet, despite her lowly place in the animal kingdom, the shock of seeing Belle's sprawled-out, limp body splayed across her soiled wood chips changed something inside of me. Not in a dark and twisty Dr. Meredith Grey kind of way, but in the way that suggested maybe I wasn't the pet-owning connoisseur I had made myself out to be during my quarterly "Buy me a puppy" trifold poster presentations in our living room.

Let me back up. For years, my three younger siblings and I had been lobbying hard for a family dog.

"We'll take care of it!" we promised.

"We'll walk it!" we pleaded.

"We won't let it starve and die!" we lied.

Our latest attempt at persuasion had been creating elaborate poster presentations for our parents to suffer through, perhaps in hopes of boring them into a state of puppy-buying submission. The posters were your standard elementary school science project fare, covered top to bottom in grainy black-and-white computer printouts of random clip art dogs and pie charts that represented how the four of us would divide the puppy caretaking duties.

Kelly:
Walking: 20 percent
Feeding: 20 percent
Pooper Scooper: 10 percent

Mark:
Walking: 35 percent
Feeding: 35 percent
Pooper Scooper: 45 percent

Jack:
Walking: 35 percent
Feeding: 35 percent
Pooper Scooper: 45 percent

Even my sister Christine, who was just a toddler at the time, was given a wedge on the charts, not because we wanted to be nice and include her, but because my dad was infamous for giving her cash for being cute, so we knew she'd be an asset to the cause.

Christine:
Walking: 10 percent
Feeding: 10 percent

Doing cartwheels and other cute three-year-old stuff so
Dad will buy us all exactly what we want: 80 percent

I'm not sure exactly what it was about our presentations that didn't land with our parents. I had used all my dad's best office supplies for the task, and yet they still maintained their united front of *no,* reminding us that dogs were a lot more responsibility than just feeding and walking. And we'd be surprised by just how much of our time and attention a dog would require. The wildly false claims they were making about pet ownership made absolutely no sense to the four of us. The entire bedrock of our presentation was the division-of-labor pie charts, and from that we would not be shaken. Unless . . . maybe our parents needed to see it all in bar-graph form. . . .

But before we could run off and waste another full ream of Hammermill computer paper with those little holes on the side that you had to tear off *juuuust* so, my parents came up with a counterproposal. In an effort to show us what real dog ownership was like and also to dissuade us from any future living room presentations, they offered to schlepp all of us to PetSmart to pick out our very own starter pets (also known as caged vermin)—and a betta fish for Christine.

We arrived at the decidedly not-PETA-friendly pet superstore and elbowed each other all the way to the automatic front doors that blasted our olfactory senses with the smell of wet fur and iguana food as soon as they opened. Completely unfazed, the four of us wandered the aisles of the pet store, our chins dragging on the dog-hair-covered floor. Never had we entered a place like this—with the intention of picking out an animal of our very own. Oh, the possibilities! Would we choose a mouse or a gerbil or a hamster or a ferret or a rabbit, or the holy grail of all caged childhood pets, a guinea pig?

Mark and Jack quickly settled on pets of the tiny variety: a hamster and a gerbil, respectively. My brothers, who shared a room as human beings, saw no reason the rodent extensions of themselves should require their own habitats. And so it was decided the hamster and the gerbil would live together in one tiny cage, defying the laws of nature, as well as the recommendations of the dead-behind-the-eyes PetSmart employee who emphatically suggested each animal be allowed its own living space.

While my brothers were off selecting plastic balls of varying sizes so their pets could "get exercise," I was homing in on my final selection. According to the laminated flap of paper zip-tied to her cage, the object of my desire was a two-toned, female guinea pig named Aretha. I was drawn to her because she wasn't balled up in a heap with all the other guinea pigs who were making a sort of quivering pig pile in one corner of the cage. She was an outside-the-box kind of guinea pig, and I liked that about her.

She was a rebel.

Once we arrived back home, I could not wait to hustle up to my room and get Belle situated. I *had* to change her name to Belle because Belle was the best Disney princess, and because I now had the best guinea pig, it seemed like an obvious decision. I couldn't wait for all the fun we were going to have—Belle and me. Late-night snuggle sessions. Me building mazes for her out of all my stuffed animals. It was going to be the cutest thing anyone had ever seen. As I started up the steps, with Belle doing her little guinea pig–style grunts in excitement, I heard my mother's voice calling to me from the kitchen. She was refilling Christine's betta fish tank with tap water, as nine-tenths of it had sloshed out while we were driving home. That poor fish didn't stand a chance.

"Kelly! Those animals live in the basement! Your brothers are already down there. Go help them get set up."

The basement? With the boys and their filthy, budget mice? This was not what Belle and I were about. She was going to be so disappointed. (Mostly because she ends up dying at the end of this story, but also because she was going to have to share a room with boys. Gross.) I plodded down the stairs to our basement playroom, Belle's cage bouncing off my shins with each disgruntled step. The boys had already dropped their cage in the back storage room and loaded their pets into their plastic exercise balls. For their part, both the hamster and the gerbil had taken massive, pellet-style dumps inside said exercise balls, creating a sort of "pooping lawn-mower toy" effect as they ran around the tiled basement floor.

Sick.

I was so glad to have chosen the most refined member of the rodent family as my ward. Belle would never poo inside a ball and run around in it. She was a lady.

The room where the new pets would stay was essentially the hallway to the unfinished storage area of our basement. It was flanked on either side by a door leading back to our play area and a bulkhead that led directly out to our backyard, and ten-degree New England winters. The hallway didn't have a light per se, but if you left the playroom door slightly ajar, the animals would not be forced to live in eternal night and might even have access to a smidge of our house's central heat. It certainly wasn't the cushy setup I would have provided in the luxury of my bedroom, but I reasoned that didn't really matter because I was planning to spend every waking moment downstairs playing with Belle, all as a part of my genius plot to show my parents their stupid plan to teach us responsibility was a farce, and they should just buy us a puppy already.

For the first few ~~months weeks~~ days of Belle's time with us, I did exactly as I had planned. I scrambled down to the basement first thing every morning to check on her and refresh her food and water. I tousled her fur and said really cool, petownery things like, "Who's my special girl?" and "Are you the best little piggy wiggy in the whole wide world?" I was going to forge a superspecial bond with Belle that I was sure my parents would notice. If they weren't going to get me a puppy, then they were going to have to listen to me talk incessantly about this guinea pig until all our brains liquefied.

What I didn't account for at the time—because I was

eleven—was that I was eleven. And because I was eleven, I had the bandwidth of, let's say, a small rodent. After a couple of weeks of doting on my new furry friend, the allure of the whole thing waned so drastically that I started to forget about Belle altogether. I know, it's an awful rookie mistake, and not at all the image of myself I had carefully curated in my Lisa Frank journal. But in my defense, she did absolutely nothing memorable, so in a way it was kind of her fault. I doubt I would've forgotten about her if she had, for instance, caught a Frisbee in her mouth or licked my face every day after school, but no. She just made her grunty little guinea pig noises and drank from her little water bottle and that was it.

My visits with Belle became less and less frequent. I'd scoot downstairs to fill her water and food before school, shutting the door completely when I left. And by the time I got home from the drudgery of fifth grade, I simply couldn't be bothered to look up from my Funyuns long enough to join my brothers in playing with the pets our parents had spent *tens* of dollars buying us. Had someone thought to call the ASPCA, I wouldn't have even blamed them. But it's not like I was actively attempting to neglect my pet; it's just that I forgot to continue to care about her, which one might argue could've been due to my teetering on the edge of pubescence and not because I was a burgeoning serial killer.

Puberty aside, Belle's well-being eventually ceased to exist on my radar—at all. I'd love to sugarcoat the ending to this story, but the animal rights people would see through it anyway, so I'm just going to lay it all out on the table. The truth of the matter was that I completely stopped feeding Belle and giving her water for, honestly, I don't even know how many days. Each morning I'd think, *I'll check on her after school,* and each afternoon I'd rationalize, *I'll check on her in the morning.* And because she was my responsibility, no one else was looking in the storage area to make sure my furry little piggy was being taken care of in any capacity. It was awful. I still feel bad about it. Even right now, this very second, as I type these words while watching *The Golden Girls* reruns on Hulu.

So the poor thing died. She kicked the bucket. Went to the great big exercise ball in the sky.

It wasn't until my friend Laura came to hang out over the weekend and I wanted to show off my "beloved" pet, whom I cared about so deeply, that I found/smelled Belle stiff and splayed out on the floor of her cage in the dark. It was a grim scene, and walking in on it did not feel good. Especially because I knew, without a shadow of a doubt, this death was 100 percent my fault. Sure, every kid kills a pet at some point in their life—we've all flushed goldfish and buried the occasional hermit crab, but what kind of little girl cares so little about animals that she just forgets they need food and water? Punky Brewster would never.

I felt like an awful person that day. And rightly so. I was a pet murderer. Not only that, now my parents were never going to buy me a puppy! Because if you do the math, killing a guinea pig is sad, but killing a puppy is like five hundred thousand times sadder—and who wants to bring that kind of potential negativity into a household? Not Mark and Peggy Barons, I'll tell you that right now.

I contemplated backing out of the room and leaving Belle until she just disintegrated into nothingness, but that felt a little dark, even for my newfound persona of guinea pig murderer. Plus, there's no way my naturally guilty Catholic conscience could've survived keeping this mortal sin a secret. So I gave in to the urge that said, "Cry, Kelly" and let the waterworks flow. My dumbfounded friend Laura and I walked up the stairs to find my mom, who was wiping the kitchen counter while my brothers fought to the death on the couch in the living room.

"Mom, I think Belle's dead," I whimpered, oh so subtly.

"You think she's dead? Did you check?"

"Did I check? What do you mean did I check? How do you 'check' to see if something is dead?"

Here's where I should mention that my mom grew up on a large cattle ranch in rural Florida. One time, while I was visiting my relatives there, one of my uncles castrated a calf in front of me and then threw the detached testicles to the family dog, so her lack of emotional turmoil over the demise of my pet rodent was not at all surprising.

"I don't know, Mom. She just looks dead. I think she's definitely dead. Also, I forgot to feed her this week."

My mom stopped wiping the counter and turned to me with a look that I read as both "I'm sorry, sweetheart" and "I told you so" at the same time.

"Well, when your father gets home, he can help you deal with it." Loosely translated, that meant, "When your father gets home, he will scoop Belle up with a shovel and fling her lifeless body into the woods behind our house." Our family apparently didn't do pet funerals, which was okay because I don't know exactly what one says during a eulogy for a guinea pig—maybe something like, "She sure knew how to lick the heck out of a salt wheel."

Later that night, before my dad came home, I went back down into the small basement room where Belle still lay in her cage, and I whispered a little apologetic goodbye to my first pet. I like to think that wherever Belle was, she knew how sorry I felt for killing her (by accident) and she didn't hold a grudge or blame me too much for not living up to either of our expectations.

I was just a kid after all. A kid whose only real crime was not making awesome enough pie charts for her living room poster presentation. Because if you really think about it, this whole "accidental guinea pig death" thing could've been avoided if my parents would've just bought us a damn puppy.

CHAPTER 4

The Fire

The story of Job is one of the only Bible stories the Catholic Church teaches young children, in the hopes of scaring them into believing in God for fear of disgusting boils and the extermination of their entire family. This was extra frightening for me, because Job was a guy who did everything right and yet still got caught in the crossfire one time when the devil was being a total fartknocker to God. As a child who measured her self-worth according to traditional Catholic standards, it was always my assumption that if I listened to my parents, didn't steal, and never, ever engaged in "boob stuff" with boys, God and I would have some kind of an understanding that he would *not smite me.* He would save all his big and scary wrath for other, poorly behaved kids and, because I had proved myself worthy by keeping all the commandments (ask me how many times I had coveted a neighbor's wife!), I would be left alone. But the story of Job took that little misguided notion, cast it into the body of a wild hog, and ran it straight off a cliff.

Because my brother Jack was our family Job.

The second youngest of our family's four kids, Jack never made it a full calendar year without a freak accident or illness sidelining him for weeks at a time. He was eight by the time our family had identified the genetic syndrome that caused his chronic stomach and bone issues, and by then he was on a collision course for multiple knee, ankle, and shoulder surgeries before his eighteenth birthday. Legend has it that he once had to Uber himself to an emergency room after throwing his back out in college, and as far as I know, he is the only one in our family to have ever been kicked off a cruise ship for vomiting over the gangway handrail.

But because none of his various ailments ever really affected me personally, whenever he was ailing I was content to play the role of Sympathetic Sister #1: Gatorade bringer and Gameboy battery replacer. I also always made sure to step over his legs when they were in casts, a courtesy I did not extend to my other, able-bodied siblings, who could suck an egg if I needed to get by.

So frequent were Jack's incidents that the typical medical accoutrement that might become temporary fixtures in a home after a one-time surgery became indispensable in the Barons house: self-inflating, wearable ice packs; extra armpit-padding crutches; portable commodes—these were the kinds of staples you could find hiding in plain sight in our TV room. And Jack loved it. Not the being hurt part, but the "being the patient" part. When my high school girlfriends would come over to hang out after school during one of his recoveries, Jack would take that exact opportunity to wheel himself over to his portable toilet and shout that he "needed help getting on the commode!" or that he "already pooped and can't reach the toilet paper from the commode!"

It was a solid move for a third-grader and the poor kid was hard up for entertainment, so like 95 percent of the time I'd give in and bring him some toilet paper. (But not the good kind. I'd bring the single-ply my dad kept in his home office, for spite.) And I knew the other 5 percent of the time, eventually Mom would hear all the screaming and would bring Jack something to wipe with, usually with my little sister Christine tagging along behind her with her Baby Tumbles Surprise doll. As punishment for my neglectful behavior, Mom would usually shuffle Christine into wherever my friends and I were sprawled at the time and inform me that it was time to let Chrissy play with us. As if we were playing?! Geez, Mom, we were thirteen!

One late afternoon in the fall of 1999, six weeks after Jack's first knee surgery and right around the time he was able to start getting out of his wheelchair and up onto a pair of crutches, our mom decided it would be okay to leave him home with my dad while she and I ran to the store for some groceries.[1]

---

1. Sidebar: As I'm writing this, the entire free world now agrees that asking a father to "babysit" his own children is garbage, but this was the nineties and moms were the ones who knew and did all the kid-related things, so let's all just pat ourselves on the back for doing better now. End sidebar.

Because of his surgery, Jack was under strict orders from his orthopedic surgeon not to run under any circumstances (which I'd like to ask you to file away and remember for, like, three minutes from now—it'll be relevant, I promise). So while Mom and I were strolling through the aisles of Market Basket, grabbing Pop-Tarts (the best part of waking up) and Cinnamon Toast Crunch, my dad, Jack, and the rest of my siblings were left to fend for themselves as the clock ticked toward dinnertime.

It was October and the Red Sox were in the midst of yet another ill-fated playoff run. The first pitch of Game 5 of the American League Divisional Series (ALDS) was scheduled for later that night, and with the Sox's 3–1 game lead over the Cleveland Indians hanging in the balance, our whole family was giddy with excitement. Jack was no different and, to celebrate, he decided to make himself a fancy pregame snack: pepperoni and cheese Bagel Bites. This sort of luxury would typically be forbidden so close to dinnertime, but with Mom out of the house and the Sox in the postseason, the only house rule was that there were no rules!

As my dad was getting settled into his preferred game-watching chair in the living room, Jack hobbled his way into the kitchen on his crutches and yanked the five-pound Costco box of Bagel Bites out of the freezer. With the weight of his body resting on a single crutch, he shoved the giant box under his free armpit and hopped his way over to the toaster oven, which rested just beside the large sink in the front of our kitchen. Then, with all the gentleness and care of an OB/GYN delivering a fresh, new baby, Jack slid a sleeve of nine Bagel Bites out of their Costco mothership and into the toaster oven.

Around the time Mom and I were checking out at the grocery store, the timer on the toaster oven signaled that Jack's pizza bagels were ready to scald the roof of his mouth, and he glanced around for something to retrieve them with. With the oven mitts and dishcloths nestled in a drawer clear across the kitchen, Jack opted instead for something that was within arm's reach: a paper towel. His hands protected by nothing but a thin layer of Bounty, he pulled down the exterior door and reached into the 350° toaster oven, which—you guessed it!—immediately caused the paper towel to combust into a sheet of flames.

Not wanting to interrupt my father's pregame experience (or get in trouble for his terrible lapse in potholder judgment), Jack didn't make a sound. He simply began shuffling toward the back door with a ball of fire in his hand. He later told us he didn't want to throw the paper towel in the sink, because he was scared it might burn the whole house down, so he opted instead to inch his way out of the house like a wounded snail because, as you'll remember, he was instructed that under no circumstances should he attempt running of any kind. Say what you will about the Barons, but we are nothing if not a family of rule followers.

The house was no worse off, but my brother's thumb was a shell of its former self, having been burned down to a throbbing, red nub. Think Freddy Krueger's face but in thumb form. Scorched, yet confident that his act of heroism would now stave off any sort of potential punishment from our father, Jack shuffled his way over to Dad to relay what had happened and receive proper medical attention, which to my father, who had a game to watch and no wife to consult, was a bowl of ice water. This is a small but important step above "rubbing some dirt on it," and, to my father's credit, there wasn't much else that could've been done. The burn looked bad but not emergency-room bad, and Dad hadn't exactly seen the fireball burning his son's flesh, only the aftermath. So he had no way of knowing all the details, especially since Jack wasn't exactly champing at the bit to recount the fact that he'd nearly torched the kitchen.

When Mom and I walked back into the house, arms full of groceries, the whole situation had settled down to a simmer. Dad was back watching the Red Sox pregame, and Jack was sitting by himself at the kitchen counter, eating pizza bagels and soaking his thumb in a bowl of ice water.

"Why does it smell like smoke in here?" I asked as I slipped fourteen bags of groceries off my left wrist.

"Jack burned his hand on some pizza bagels," Dad called from the living room, as my mom lifted Jack's limp hand out of the cereal bowl it had been resting in. By this time Jack's thumb had begun to blister and looked more like a pus-filled caterpillar than a proper digit.

"I'm calling Mary Lou to come over and see this," Mom announced as she extended the antenna on the portable telephone. "I don't like the way it looks—or smells."

Mary Lou, our family friend and a former nurse at Shriners Hospital for Children, confirmed that Jack should be seen at a burn unit immediately. Do not stop at the pediatrician's office. Do not pass Go. Do not collect $200. So just before the Sox took the field for what would be the final game of the ALDS, Mom, Jack, and I piled into the car and drove into Boston.

Typically, attempting to drive into downtown Boston as a Red Sox playoff game was about to start would be considered a suicide mission, but Game 5 was being played 650 miles away at Jacobs Field in Cleveland, so we cruised down I-93 without the extra weight of game-day traffic. Even with his hand in poor condition, Jack insisted that we should try and listen to as much of the game as possible before arriving at Shriners. Mom and I agreed that if we were going to be in the car anyway, it would be sacrilege not to tune into Red Sox broadcasters Joe Castiglione and Jerry Trupiano's lead-in to the game. So as we drove we listened, and for the two-thirds of us in the car without severe burns, Joe and Jerry took our minds off things.

The doctors at Shriners confirmed what we had suspected: Jack had third-degree burns covering a large portion of his left hand and would need to follow a complex burn protocol for the next several weeks to help minimize any permanent damage. By the time we piled back into the car several hours later with the majority of Jack's hand covered in medical gauze of varying thicknesses, Pedro Martinez was already shocking the forty-five thousand people at Jacob's Field by coming out of the bullpen in stellar relief, and my second-favorite player, left fielder Troy O'Leary, had clubbed a grand slam in the third. As we drove north on I-93 toward home, the Sox and Indians were tied up at eight runs each heading into the seventh inning.

Worn out from spending the evening at the hospital, the three of us rode in silence as we listened to Trupiano's play-by-play warble over the airwaves. Jack held his hand tenderly in his lap and stared out the backseat window into the cool October night, undoubtedly replaying the events of the day over again in his mind. Shortly after the seventh-inning stretch, the traffic on the interstate began to slow to a crawl, an oddity this late in the evening. Fighting our normal Bostonian urges to rage against this stroke of bad traffic, we chose instead to focus our energy on helping the Sox defend Pedro's chance at a big playoff win. As we channeled our good vibes to send to Cleveland, we noticed most of the drivers around us were listening to the broadcast, too, often tooting their horns in unison during particularly tense at-bats or throwing their hands up in disgust when Indians manager Mike Hargrove made the call to once again walk the extremely hot bat of Nomar Garciaparra to get to my guy, #25, O'Leary. It was like we were all sitting together in one giant, slow-rolling sports bar—minus the alcohol, of course.

The anticipation of every pitch radiated from each car, truck, and van on the highway. By now, Mom, Jack, and I had locked eyes with the drivers of both the Honda and Mazda in the neighboring lanes and felt comfortable exchanging nervous smiles and raised fists as O'Leary walked to the plate to face Paul Shuey, the Indians' right-handed reliever.

The next few moments went down as both the quietest and most uproarious in Boston highway history. There was a tense and collective silence until each car heard the magical sound of Jerry Trupiano's home-run call: "Waaaaay baaaack, grand slam, Troy O'Leary!"

Every car horn within ten miles erupted in a string of loud honks, beeps, and blasts. Semi-trailer truck drivers pulled their weird rope horn things, and motorcyclists beeped their tiny, cartoonish-sounding ones. The people in the cars around us were whooping and hollering and thrusting their fists into the air through open sunroofs and cracked windows. Even Jack, who'd barely managed a smile since we left the hospital, pounded on the back window until we worried he'd ruin the one good hand he had left. For the next thirty seconds, we were not just an exhausted family driving home from the hospital; we were a part of something much bigger—something you can only really understand if your love for baseball begins way down deep in your marrow.

When I think about it now, it's so obvious that baseball was the thing that shepherded us through this small tragedy. During what should have been a really scary and potentially traumatizing medical emergency, we got to experience the joy of something sacred that bound us together as a family. Is it supercorny to think of all the other Red Sox fans on the highway as a multitude of angels surrounding us as we drove home from the hospital? *Yes.* Does it make me feel better and suggest that maybe God looks after us using the things we care about even when real life is crappy? *Also yes.*[2]

Out of nowhere, the traffic that had held us back slowly dissipated and we began to speed up, waving goodbye to the Mazda and Honda who'd become our temporary baseball family. I felt disappointed to leave our electric, shared moment behind, but as the speedometer was finally able to inch past the seventy-miles-per-hour. mark, Jack and I set our sights on a new target: the American League Championship Series against the New York Yankees—and convincing Mom to drive through Burger King before we went home.

2. They say God moves in mysterious ways, but there are times when his moves are so on the nose (like the perfect Lifetime movie marathon when you're stuck in bed sick, or a surprise shirt in your glove compartment when your infant diarrheas through his onesie while you're breastfeeding) that you can't help but feel like, "You get me."

CHAPTER 5

One-Star Kiss

I tell most people that my first kiss happened in the seventh grade, when I was twelve. Actually, I really don't tell anyone that, because who asks a thirty-six-year-old woman about her first kiss anymore unless she's being forced to play one of those terrible introspective icebreaker games against her will? You know the kind—where players have to share feelings and past experiences in order to force workplace relationships. It's like Candyland, but for your repressed childhood trauma.

But whenever it does come up, I say seventh grade, Gabe Daniels. In my best friend's bathroom. And yes, it was a dare. What did you want me to do? Pick truth? What if they asked me about something embarrassing, like tampons? Or which animated Disney character I thought was hottest? No, thank you. I'd rather risk catching strep throat from my boyfriend of two-and-a-half months than bear the potential humiliation of having to admit I thought Timon was the sexiest animated character in *The Lion King.*

So when I was dared to stand beside a toilet and press my lips up against another human being for the first time, I jumped at the chance. I was almost a teenager—long overdue to cross the tonsil hockey threshold. And it's not like I wouldn't know what I was doing—I'd mentally made out with Jack Dawson hundreds of times. Plus, it would be private. It would be intimate. It would be right next to where my friend's family pooped and peed. I was finally growing up.

Like Wendy Moira Angela Darling walking the plank as Tick-Tock the crocodile licked his lips below, Gabe and I slowly made our way into the "make-out space" and closed the door. With our friends' ears pressed up against the outside of the door, we made awkward conversation and absolutely zero eye contact. "We don't have to do this if you don't want to," he mumbled.

We didn't? Did he not understand suburban middle school social dynamics? If we walked out of that room without little bits of each other's spittle on our lips, that would equal total humiliation. It would be all over the school by 9:00 a.m. the next day that I had refused a perfectly good opportunity for a smooch session. "Kelly Barons is a prude," everyone would write in expertly folded notes to be passed between classes, and no boy would ever ask me out. And even if I *was* a prude,

I didn't need everyone at William Diamond Middle School whispering about it over fruit cocktail in the cafeteria. I'd rather endure a one-star first-kiss experience than upend my social station.

Unfortunately, at the time, I cared more about impressing my friends than I did about respecting my own body/worth/what-I-wanted-to-do; I really wanted to just run out of that little bathroom screaming and go home to watch Rosie O'Donnell fling Koosh balls into her live studio audience.

But alas, there was to be no watching Rosie that day. I would kiss a boy instead, whether I liked it or not.

The kiss itself, as you most likely guessed, was a flop. On paper, it *was* technically a kiss, in that our mouths touched and saliva was exchanged. But if we were to roll the tape back, I think it would be physically impossible for any human being to watch the replay without cringing. Like *reeeeeeally* cringing. I mean absolutely no offense to my kissing partner, who I'm sure was understandably grossed out by my lack of expertise during the abomination that was our half-mouth-open-no-tongue slobberfest, but now that I am a grown-ass ladywoman who has twenty-plus years of kissing experience, I can firmly state, with no hesitation, that no person is physically or emotionally ready to be doing any kind of kissing while they are young enough to still be eating Dunkaroos regularly.

It bears mentioning that, at the time of our kiss, I had no less than thirty-two silver brackets on my teeth and the lingering effects of a palate expander that had spent the better part of the last year pushing my front teeth apart by way of a tiny key that I cranked every morning in front of the mirror. The state of my oral cavity alone should've precluded me from attempting any kind of kissing, but we did it anyway because we had been "boyfriend/girlfriend" for ten whole weeks, and it seemed like the next logical relationship step after he and I had written, "I love you" and "P.S. I love you," respectively, in each other's yearbooks on the bus earlier that day. The "P.S." part was because I didn't write it to him until I saw that he had scrawled it all over my yearbook on the bus earlier that day.

"Oh, I didn't finish mine!" I said, snatching his yearbook back out of his hands. It was . . . so smooth.

I also think a little piece of me knew that this would be our last-ever written correspondence. He was never going to write to me after he left for his summerlong sleepaway camp—even though he had sworn he would (in Gelly Roll pen) in my yearbook. It was a coed camp, and the rumor mill on the bat mitzvah circuit that year was that, apparently, sleepaway camp girls let boys see their bras. Their bras! My bra still triggered a shame response when I put it on every morning, so I was not about to let another human being look at it—especially not a boy. Sick! What would he even do with it? Wear it like a hat? Shoot frogs out of it like a slingshot? I was clueless.

Because the laws of adolescence told me that Gabe would probably be making out with some bra-showing girl from the next cabin the whole freaking summer, I figured we'd better face-smash while we had the chance. I didn't want to miss my chance at a kiss with Gabe because some floozy at arts and crafts beat me to it. How dare she? It didn't occur to me at the time that I was slut-shaming some poor, unnamed girl, instead of, I don't know, expecting my boyfriend to be faithful? I blame the little devil on my shoulder[1] for whispering, *But how could we expect a boy to be faithful if he sees a bra, Kelly? And a real one too; not like the gross, unlined "junior" ones you pick out of a bin at Marshall's.*

Against all middle school relationship odds, Gabe proved me wrong. He *did* write me letters from camp, but he also totally sucked face with some girl from the next cabin. When I later found out about his lack of fidelity, I imagined him sitting on the camp's dock, locking lips with the girl with the cute bra, while literally writing a letter to me behind her back. While the physics of that obviously don't make sense, neither does cheating on your perfectly innocent, brace-faced girlfriend who is sitting back in Lexington, Massachusetts gagging every time she has to return a letter with "I love you" written in it.

Greater romances have been through far greater tragedies, but Gabe's duplicity was one of the great injustices of my young dating life. Even though I later banded a group of middle school girls together to shun Gabe Daniels and swear on a stack of *Sweet Valley High* books that they'd never go out with him, I can't say I was really all that broken up about his betrayal. Because the truth was, he wasn't really my first kiss at all. My first kiss had happened five years before, sitting in a

1. For the sake of naming him, let's just call him, oh, I don't know, Purity Culture Carl?

computer chair in my second-grade classroom, while I played the original Mac version of Oregon Trail. That day, my friend Andrew Foster kissed me on the top of my head, right after I had died of dysentery.

Now that is what I'd call a five-star kiss.

CHAPTER 6

Trigger Warning: Intrusive Thoughts

In the Catholic Church, the first few years of religious education are spent preparing young boys and girls to make their first confession. If you're unfamiliar, confession is when you sit with your parish priest and verbally list all the bad things you've done or thought or thought about thinking about. The idea being, your priest will act as an intermediary between you and God and offer you a chance to complete your penance to atone for your sins, and thus be granted God's complete forgiveness—until you inevitably mess up again and have to go back to confession.

It usually went a little something like this:

CHILD: "Forgive me, Father, for I have sinned. This is my first confession."

PRIEST: "Continue, my child."

CHILD: "Um, okay. Well, I hit my brother forty-three times. I yelled at my sister for touching my stuff every single day this week. I think I thought about my neighbor dying in a car crash, but I'm not sure. I stole a Coke from the fridge after my mom said not to. I think there was other stuff too, but I forget. I am sorry for all my sins."

FATHER: *Prays the Prayer of Absolution, makes the sign of the cross, and prescribes three Hail Marys and two Acts of Contrition.*

CHILD: *Prays prayers.* BOOM! FORGIVEN.

Now listen, I am not here to pick apart the religiosity and tradition of the Catholic Church or any church; however, *steps on soap box* if religious bodies are going to teach generation after generation of children to believe their worth and the destination of their eternal souls is tied to their performance during their literal *first try* at being a human being, there's going to be some pretty traumatic fallout.

For me that fallout looked like crippling, intrusive thoughts and clinical diagnosis of obsessive-compulsive disorder (OCD) at the ripe old age of eleven. So cute, right? It was the *best*! My favorite part of being a kid was waking up in the morning and accidentally thinking about what would happen if I burned my house down. It was such a magical time. If you're a person who struggles with intrusive thoughts, you know they usually stem from your worst-case scenarios. And when your entire religious upbringing centers around avoiding being the cause of worst-case scenarios, you come up with some pretty gnarly ones. But before we really dive into this conversation, please don't hear me saying that the Catholic Church is responsible for my mental illness; it merely shaped its presentation.

The whole thing started pretty innocuously. I worried about us having enough gas in our family car or making sure my bladder was *completely* empty before I left the house—not exactly huge red flags or the textbook OCD symptoms anyone had seen in *What About Bob?* or *As Good as It Gets,* the cultural touchstones for all things mental illness in the nineties. So my parents just let it ride. My worrying would flare up from time to time, but overall it was nothing too concerning, considering how weird kids are in general. Like if my parents were going to get all worked up over these seemingly benign fears, then they'd also have to have some misgivings about the fact that I was performing a full-length version of *Jesus Christ Superstar,* in which I played Jesus, Mary Magdalene, Judas, and Peter, in the middle of our living room every single afternoon.

That all changed around the time my youngest sister, Christine, was born. Somewhere between my time spent thinking about Sully from *Dr. Quinn, Medicine Woman* and debating which was better, the live-action *Flintstones* film or the original Hanna-Barbera made-for-TV cartoon, I started thinking about . . . other stuff. Other weird stuff. What kind of weird stuff? Well . . .

I worried that when I walked to the gas station across the street from our house I might purposely step in old gasoline and track it back to my house and then light a match and burn the house to the ground with my family inside.

I worried that I might purposely push my best friend into traffic when I invited her over to my house to play.

I worried that I might purposely kick someone in the head while I was swinging on our swing set.

Of course, I never, ever did any of those things. Or anything close to them. But still I worried that I might, and wouldn't that make me a bad person? The thoughts began to get so frightening that I would wake up every morning and try to create a version of white noise inside my own head to block out any thoughts for as long as I could, which usually wasn't even long enough to make it down to the breakfast table.

As my worries began to escalate and become more and more bizarre, so did my behavior. When we talked about this experience years later, my mom would tell me she remembered seeing me put myself in harm's way to avoid hurting people, doing things like jumping off a really high swing if another kid even entered our backyard, or making sure I walked out in the middle of the road while a friend walked safely on the sidewalk. Seeing me in action around that time was probably akin to watching Devon Sawa in *Final Destination*—except no one was *actually* about to be impaled by a log falling off the back of a truck.

Out of sheer desperation, I did discover two respites for my brain during this time:

a. If I watched *The Sound of Music* or *Full House*, I could escape my otherwise nonstop intrusive thoughts.
b. If I confessed my thoughts to my mom, I would feel "absolved."

I can only assume that the latter came from my experience with my first holy confession. When you combine that with the fact that before we knew its proper name, we called my mental illness a "guilty conscience," it's no wonder that my need for forgiveness ballooned faster than Violet Beauregarde in Willy Wonka's factory. It wasn't enough for me to acknowledge that I hadn't *actually* done anything wrong myself; I needed someone else to tell me I wasn't doing anything to feel bad about. I stopped trusting my own experience in the world, and the lines between reality and what was going on inside my head became very, very blurry.

By the time I'd reached middle school, I was calling my mom collect[1] from the pay phone outside the gym several times

1. Remember collect calls? Actually, forget collect calls. Remember long-distance phone service commercials? MCI should be ashamed of the emotional manipulation they employed trying to get a generation of adults to feel bad about not calling home enough.

every single day to confess all the terrible things I "might" have done or thought. The calls would sound something like

"You have a collect call from . . . *I cheated on my social studies test. I think I brushed up against an eighth-grader in the hallway on purpose. I thought about wanting my boobs to grow. I maybe thought about the librarian dying. I think I—*"

My mom knew better than to accept the call. There was nothing she could say. As a mom myself now, I can't even imagine how it felt to hear those things (and worse) come out of her daughter's mouth. But we had developed a rhythm: I would spew black bile from my soul and she would listen, without flinching. Sometimes I'd leave some of my confessions written in unintelligible chicken scratch on her pillow or whisper them to her while she was making dinner, and in return she would write me a sweet note using a piece of my dolphin stationery or give me a squeeze while she mashed up a meatloaf with two-thirds of a bottle of Heinz 57. But never once—not one single time—do I remember her making me feel ashamed or embarrassed about what I said. Oh sure, at times she seemed exasperated or stressed, times when I'd creep into her room late at night to confess something while she was sitting up late, literally reading the textbooks she'd checked out of the Emerson Hospital Research Library to help her make sense of what the *heck* was going on with her daughter. But she never, ever said anything to make me feel like anything less than her regular old Kelly.

We limped along like this for a while, me confessing and my mom listening. It was hell on both of us, but I dulled the pain with Maria von Trapp and the *Full House* gang and assumed, "This is my life now. It sucks, but at least I'm not Kimmy Gibbler."

I was thirty-three years old before I learned there were others like me out there. That there were other kids who woke up one morning and felt completely unable to get out of bed. That other kids sat in psychiatrists' waiting rooms listening to tiny noise machines, wondering if their next Prozac dosing would be the one that fixed everything. And I could tell you that all those experiences made me feel really alone. That I suffered with my OCD and intrusive thoughts for twenty-one years before I felt accepted or normal. And that would make for a very interesting backstory, but it would be completely untrue.

Because I never, ever felt alone or broken or sick for one very specific reason: my parents. They supported the ever-loving heck out of me, and that is the kind of grace every child deserves. There is not a day that goes by that I don't feel grateful that my parents didn't kowtow to the stigma of mental illness in the nineties or shame me because some of my intrusive thoughts were sex-based. Instead of just trying to make the OCD go away, they fought to help me become myself again, in whatever way served me best. I still get verklempt anytime I think too much about it. I mean, they went to the *library*, you guys! And got *textbooks*! Made of *paper*! I was so privileged to walk through this dark time with their encouragement, especially because even though it should be, we all know this is not the story of every child who struggles with mental illness.

Slowly, my collect calls became more and more infrequent, so much so that I don't remember batting an eyelash when our school eventually removed all the pay phones in favor of making kids call home from the supervised front office. I still feel the need to confess from time to time, even now as an adult. It's something I'm working toward outgrowing by the time I turn sixty, but my hopes are not high. Because that's how mental illness works—it waxes and wanes like the moon.[2] Some days are good, others are not. I remember my psychiatrist telling me as much from her chair in her small office at Boston Children's Hospital—that things would never truly be all-the-way better, which is a little scary to think about as a pre-teen. But really, mental illness or not, are any of us ever all-the-way better? Or are we just constantly ebbing and flowing through life like the tides,[3] with some days more difficult than others?

There was a story that came out not that long ago about a Boston lobsterman who was nearly swallowed by a humpback whale while he was diving to check on some of his lobster traps. Apparently, the whale scooped him up like a piece of human krill and held him inside his mouth for a minute or so before spitting him back to the land of the living. During a news interview immediately after his close encounter, the lobsterman likened getting swallowed by the whale to being "hit by a truck" and that the inside of the whale's mouth felt "hard all around." He went on to say that after a few terrifying

---

2. Does anyone *really* know which direction is "waxing" and which is "waning"? I mean besides seventh-grade earth science teachers . . .
3. Again, not sure which way is which.

moments of wondering if he was about to live or die, he saw a light at the front of the whale's mouth, and almost instantly the whole experience was over.

A week after that story hit the news, my sister Christine was in LA, where she lives now, hanging out at the Roosevelt Hotel pool, when a man with a heavy Boston accent started chatting with her. He was in LA for the first time with his wife because Jimmy Kimmel had invited him onto his late-night talk show.

"Why?" my sister asked.

"Because I'm the guy that got swallowed by the whale!" he boasted, proud as you please, before returning to join his wife on their lounge chairs. Now this might seem like a weird, name-drop-y story,[4] but it might also seem, at its core, to be a story about how a person can go from arguably the darkest, hardest moment in their life, to the total opposite, which according to my calculations is having a superfun pool day with your partner in sunny California.

Life's never going to be "all-the-way" better, but it's also not going to eat you alive.

4. Does it count as name-drop-y if it's about my sister meeting a guy who met a famous guy? I sort of feel like I'm in the clear here.

CHAPTER 7

An Ox with Braces

Being a good girlfriend can be exhausting, especially when we're living in such a polarizing time. Especially when we are expected to be so many things to so many people. And *especially* after we've all experienced the collective trauma of trying to make Zoom cocktails a thing.

We've become a generation of women who are drained by the responsibility of friendship.

In fact, if you were to put all the responsibilities of friendship down on paper, I would wager that it would end up longer than all the stories your kid tells you about Minecraft put together. I mean, you've got the basics like

1. being nice,
2. supporting each other,
3. texting back,
4. remembering birthdays, and
5. noticing haircuts.

But then you've got to keep in mind all the nuanced pieces of twenty-first-century friendship, like

1. sending topical memes,
2. knowing emotional triggers,
3. gauging her multilevel marketing preferences,
4. knowing which type of feminine hygiene product she might need in a pinch, and
5. being aware of her stance on Pinterest board collaboration.

It's so much to keep straight, which may be why a large portion of us were somewhat thankful to be relieved of a lot of social responsibilities during this century's global pandemic.

You mean I can hit "pause" on attending large gatherings of people and making chitchat for a full calendar year? I'm not seeing a downside here. . . .

And, of course, someone would explain the downside and you would be like, "Oh my God, really?" and they would be like, "Yeah." And you would be like, "Oh man, no thanks."

And then they would be like, "Too late, you already signed up for the pandemic." And you'd be like, "Crap."

Because we never knew how unprepared we were for friendshipping during whatever the heck 2020 was, mostly because so many adult friendships are way more fragile than we realized, and many of them just weren't strong enough to withstand month after month of *Airplane!*-style slaps in the face from current events. It's hard enough to maintain a friendship when you don't share the same stance on your favorite Kardashian (Kim, duh). But what happens when you don't agree on your president? Or vaccines? Or religion? Does this automatically mean you snuff out your friendship altogether? Kick 'em to the curb? Put the kibosh on the whole shebang?

A little piece of me wanted to say "yes." Set boundaries. Delete your friendship cache. Get rid of the people who don't make you feel like your best self. But then I remembered something that happened back when I was a butterfly-clip-wearing middle schooler, and I committed one of the most egregious Girl Code violations on record.

It was the night of one of our school dances, and the hormones of two hundred sweaty pre-teens hung over our middle school gymnasium like a mushroom cloud. My girlfriends and I had congregated at my house beforehand to apply glitter to our temples, slick back our ponytails, and give my mom our Domino's order for postdance pizza.

While we were getting ready in my bathroom, Jen, one of my very best friends, was going on and on about how she really wanted this guy Dave to ask her to dance. Dave was okay—not really all that cute in my opinion,[1] but Jen really liked him. Standard 1998 predance hype protocol dictated that our other friend, Anna, and I assure her that Dave would *totally* ask her to dance, while we took turns spritzing her with lethal amounts of Gap Dream perfume. They returned the favor by telling me that the guy I really liked, Evan, would *totally* ask me to dance too. We were all *totally* going to dance with our dream guys! It was going to be *totally* perfect! And we were all going to smell *totally* dreamy!

At 6:59 p.m. we clamored out of my mom's spruce-green Mazda MPV and literally sprinted into the school gym. That was the beauty of middle school dances. You were ready to bump and grind like an adult, but you were still enough of a little kid to run fast because you were excited.

Once we were inside, Jen, Anna, and I handed our xeroxed dance tickets to eighth-grade student council members who wouldn't even look us in the eye, and then—it was all happening. Right there between the PE locker rooms and carts of semi-inflated kickballs. We danced with abandon to the *Space Jam* soundtrack and every radio-edit hit from Puff Daddy. We got really sweaty doing the Macarena and the Electric Slide, and giggled when our drama teacher tried to join in. Between

1. His hair did NOT do the JTT thing in front, so like, that's a hard pass from me.

trips to the water fountain to guzzle mouthfuls of water like we'd been participating in an NBA game, Anna and I started hassling Jen about Dave. If he wasn't going to ask her to dance, then she should ask him. What did she have to lose? Like the writing on the wall at Limited Too always said, GiRl PoWeR!!! But despite all our amazing hype work, Jen refused, saying if Dave wanted to dance with her, then he would ask. Like the card game I was looking forward to playing during our sleepover after the dance, I called B.S. Or maybe I said "bull-crap," because what if one of the teachers heard?

Empowered by my own psych-up speech to Jen, I lumbered over to Dave like an ox with braces, to demand he dance with my friend. How dare he ignore her when she was over there looking so cute in her brand-new *Animaniacs* long-sleeved T-shirt? I saw him looking at me as I made my approach. Just then "I'll Make Love to You" or "Nice and Slow" or some other equally sexual slow jam started blaring over the speakers.

"Wanna dance?" he asked me.

"Um, sure," I answered. But only for a minute—and just to ask him about Jen. Because I was *such* a good friend.

The song droned inappropriately on and I did bring up Jen. Dave very politely said he would ask her to dance, but that he just liked her as a friend. I said, "Okay."

And then he asked me out. And I said, "Okay."

I said okay.

After the song ended, I wandered back to Anna and Jen to report what had happened with a huge smile plastered on my face. "He asked me out!" I screamed over the music.

"What?!" was their perfectly appropriate and loud reply. "How could you do that?"

"Well, he obviously likes me and not Jen. How is that my fault?" I said without a glimmer of self-awareness, slowly turning away to do The Sprinkler with some other friend before Jen and Anna could continue harshing my mellow.

After my betrayal, the rest of the night didn't go so well. News of my backstabbiness spread through the gym like lice at a slumber party—fast and mostly to girls. In the end I went home alone to eat pizza for three and sulk over the fact that I was being so wrongly persecuted for looking cute now that my palate expander had been removed. It was *so unfair.*

Dave and I ended up going out for one single, not-very-magical week, at the end of which he had Evan (remember him?) call me and break up with me. #Karma, amIright? But here's the thing: Even though I was terrified that Jen was going to stay mad indefinitely, which she had every right to do, she and all the other seventh-grade girls I had offended on her behalf forgave me. They let me know I had screwed up and broken their trust, but they didn't write me off forever because I promised to change my ways. Before long, we were sitting at the same cafeteria tables again, eating square pizza from Styrofoam trays, and planning the team spirit outfits for our next away soccer game.

When I feel a strain in a friendship or have the urge to excommunicate people I feel at odds with, sometimes I remember this story. (Other times I act like a butthead and think I'm a superior being, but let's not focus on that.) Kids have this natural conflict-resolution strategy preloaded inside them. Without ever having to be taught, my middle school friends set boundaries and expectations for our friendship moving forward, and I respected them because I learned what kind of friend they needed me to be. That's how healthy friendships work. Of course, I'm not saying it should be mandatory that we always let people who hurt us stay in our lives, but when it's possible, keeping space for them to show up and try again gives people a reason to grow and change.

Offering people an opportunity to ask for forgiveness and show up for you in the way you need them to allows for our Responsibilities of Friendship list to become a whole lot shorter, and I for one prefer it that way.

Responsibilities of Friendship

1. Respect each other.
2. No more Zoom cocktails.

CHAPTER 8

Sex Negative

I believe, deep down in my bones, that the conceptualization of the groundbreaking MTV reality series *The Real World* was conceived by producers Bunim and Murray themselves during a nineties-era sleepover. I know the timeline and logistics of that don't exactly track, but the similarities are too striking to ignore. Just tweak a few of the lines of *The Real World*'s original opening narration and you've got the perfect voiceover for every sleepover I attended from 1993 to 2003:

This is the true story of seven frenemies, picked to sleep in a house, gossip together, and eat a breakfast they're not like, totally comfortable with—all while being taped. Find out what happens when people stop being polite and start getting real . . . The Real World: SLEEPOVER!

Cut to: Me in my childhood bedroom, Backstreet Boys blaring. My tongue is out in deep concentration as I attempt to defy the laws of physics and squeeze a human-size sleeping bag into a canvas drawstring bag barely big enough to hold a large bunch of grapes, all while this voiceover plays:

Yeah, I guess I'm pretty excited about this sleepover. I'm looking forward to seeing everybody at the house and learning a little bit more about myself. What am I nervous about? Well, sometimes I have to pee in the middle of the night, and I don't want to flush and accidentally wake anyone up. And I'm a little bit worried about what we're going to be having for dinner. Usually, my mom lets me make a cheese sandwich if I don't like what we're having, and I don't really know what the rules are about that at this house. Oh, and I'm really not looking forward to changing into pajamas in front of everyone. I have this new training bra, but I think maybe I'll just wear it the whole time so no one sees me putting it back in my backpack. I'm not sure. I guess it'll be neat to see if anyone else has a training bra or thoughts on boobs in general. I don't really like mine, but boobs in general seem to be fueling a lot of the hot goss at school, so that's been a whole thing. Yeah, I guess you could say I have a lot of hesitations going into this experience, but, um, mostly I'm excited. I think.

Cut to: Me and my friends arriving at the designated sleepover location. Each of us being reminded via shouts from a rolled-down driver's-side window about the pickup scenario for the following morning or other borderline embarrassing tidbits of information:

"Kelly, ride with Sarah to soccer."

"Kate, your dad's picking you up at 9:30 for his weekend."

"Stephanie, don't forget to use your inhaler!"

"Dana, brush your teeth. I'm gonna check!"

Kelly confessional: *I mean, honestly, yeah, I was a little sad to see my mom drive away, okay? I mean, we usually watch* TGIF *as a family on Friday nights, so it's emotional for me to miss out on that. Plus, Anna's older brother is here tonight with some of his high school friends, and they're like cute or whatever, so now I don't really feel comfortable choreographing a dance in the living room like we had planned. Now we're probably going to have to make up the dance in Anna's bedroom, and there's just not enough room for cartwheels in there.*

Cut to: The taillights of our parents' cars moving down the driveway as we make our way to the front door to be greeted by our host's enthusiastic mom. She's smiling and letting us know we can "head on upstairs" before whispering that we'll need to "keep it down" because she's having her girlfriends over for Bunco tonight.

Kelly confessional: *Was I upset to hear that we wouldn't be able to play the Casio keyboard at full volume while we talked about starting a band? Yeah, absolutely. It's just really stressful. I'm thinking about calling my mom to come get me, if I can think of a believable enough excuse. Does "My ankle feels weird" seem believable?*

Cut to: Me and all my friends trying to get through one

take of our dance routine to Mariah Carey's *Fantasy* without someone making a passive-aggressive comment. The tension is building, because I'm insisting the routine needs at least six roundoffs and not everyone can do a roundoff. Dana and Kate can barely do a basic cartwheel, and Stephanie thinks roundoffs are stupid all of a sudden. Anna says she doesn't care either way, but I can tell she does. Right before I'm about to suggest that I just do all six roundoffs myself, Anna's mom yells up to us that the Domino's guy just dropped off our pizza.

Kelly confessional: *I'm so excited to eat pizza. Sometimes people comment about how much pizza I can eat, but I just love it so much. Um, yeah, it does make me feel weird when people say stuff about how much I like to eat, because I used to have to buy like, the biggest kids' clothes possible before I put myself on a diet way back in fifth grade, so when there's boys around and stuff I usually don't eat as much pizza as I want. But yeah, um, to answer your question, I love pizza.*

Cut to: All the girls sitting on top of their sleeping bags eating pizza and watching *Can't Hardly Wait*. We all agree that we wish we looked like Jennifer Love Hewitt and that there couldn't possibly be anything better than high school boys wanting to make out with us based on how great we looked in a blue spaghetti-strap tank top. We also spend a few minutes discussing how weird it is that you can't see her bra straps. Because isn't that why most girls wear a T-shirt under their tank tops? So you can't see their bra straps?

Kelly confessional: *I'm pretty confused about the whole bra-straps thing. I know it's really bad if they're showing, but like, how do you get them to not show unless you're wearing a full T-shirt too? And I guess I'm starting to think that maybe this whole training-bra thing isn't so bad. I mean, yeah, it's insanely uncomfortable and I'm still not really sure what the bra is training me and my boobs to do, but there doesn't seem like there's any way out of spending the rest of my life in this fabric prison, so fingers crossed I get used to it.*

Cut to: All of us girls comparing boob sizes in the bathroom mirror and talking about which one of us might get our Period first, which was almost certainly based purely on boob size.

Kelly confessional: *It's really weird to talk about our Periods. Isn't that, like, super private? I mean, it has to do with our privates, so why are we talking about it? Although I do have a lot of questions that no one has ever addressed with me, like "What is a Period?" and "Is there a way I could die from it?" Also, "Can I skip it sometimes, and if so, how?" I know we talked about it a little bit in Sex Ed, but all I remember is a video where a girl's backpack is open and like a million tampons fall out. Is that the Period?*

Cut to: Lights out. All the girls are in sleeping bags, propped up on our elbows, ready to dish out some completely fabricated and totally judgmental middle school gossip. We go around in a circle, naming girls from school and talking about their various body parts and how far we think they've gone with their boyfriends. We openly call them names if we think they've gone "too far," although admittedly some of us don't really even know what "getting to third base" means.

Some of us cling to our virtue by announcing that we'd never have sex before marriage; others tell us we're crazy and we'll change our minds. We argue over what "counts as sex" and laugh because it's all just so gross and weird, and who would ever want to put *that, there?!*

Kelly confessional: *I swear to God I will never have sex before I get married. That's just bad. It's really, really bad. Plus, what if my parents ever found out? I would die. I would just actually die. Honestly, I think I'm only ever going to have sex to make my kids, and I want to have four kids, so that means I'll only have to have sex four times.*

Cut to: It's the morning after, 7:45. The morning sun peeks in through the windows and, like Anne Hathaway emerging from her nerd cocoon in *The Princess Diaries,* we all wake up and slip out of our sleeping bags—except for the one "Sleeping Late Is My Personality" friend, who rolls over in disgust and dramatically pulls her pillow over her head. I go into the bathroom to put on my soccer uniform and look in the mirror to adjust my ultratight athletic headband. My reflection assures me that when I get to the field, my mom will say I look tired and, "We're never doing sleepovers before a game again," but for the moment I'm just grateful that we're going to have orange slices at the field, because I can smell Canadian bacon cooking in my friend's kitchen, and everyone knows that's the worst kind of bacon.

Kelly confessional: *I'd say, yeah, I'm glad I came to this sleepover. I think I learned a lot about myself, like the fact that even though I do have boobs, I'm not a slut, and neither is*

Jennifer Love Hewitt, I don't think. I also think it's pretty cool that the thoughts and opinions that I have now about my body and sex and all that gross stuff will never change, and I'll always be this exact same person in every way. That feels like a nice, safe line in the sand. Me and then waaaaaaay over there in the distance is a line and then waaaaaay on the other side of the line, is sex.

Roll credits.

CHAPTER 9

Smirnoff Sprints

As a brief social experiment, I would like to see a show of hands for everyone who grew up playing sports and believes their talents were mismanaged by a high school coach.

I'll wait.

. . .

Ah, yes. Just as I suspected.

If I had to guess, I would bet, if asked, 67 percent[1] of high school student-athletes believe at least one of their coaches was intentionally trying to sabotage their athletic career, a

1. I made up that percentage, but I'm like 97 percent sure it's accurate.

sentiment that only increases the further removed one gets from actually playing organized sports.

And it doesn't matter that most high school coaches are generally good folks just trying to tack on an extra $15,000 to their unjustifiably low teacher's salary so their family can take that summer trip to Disney World. Or that the idea of a grown person purposefully trying to "take down" a high school student is utterly ludicrous. We self-important former student-athletes just can't stand the idea that not everyone believes we are our generation's Derek Jeter or Michael Jordan or Mia Hamm or whatever other sports superstar from your youth really resonates with you.

I am not exempt from this phenomenon.

My junior year in high school, I was the starting catcher for the school's varsity softball team. We were a competitive team, by New England athletic standards, which I've since learned doesn't amount to diddly-squat in contrast to athletic standards in the South. So please don't come for me, SEC states. It also bears mentioning that not only were we decently good, but we also wore visors before softball visors really became a thing, and I would like that noted in my epitaph.

R.I.P.
Kelly Bandas
Beloved wife, mother, and softball visor early adopter
"I told you I was going to die"

As both a semiprofessional comedian *and* a hypochondriac, I have made it very clear to my husband Brian that should he choose to leave that final quotation off my headstone, I will come back and haunt him by whispering WebMD diagnoses in his ear for all eternity.

But back to the absurd grandiosity of high school sports. When I was a junior, the senior girls on our team who played were very serious athletes. Think Team Iceland from *The Mighty Ducks 2,* but for girls softball and without the accents. And our coach, Coach Leslie, had made it abundantly clear that if we were *ever* going to have a chance at a run for the Massachusetts state championship, this was going to be the year. Our two best pitchers were headed off to Division I colleges after this season, and once the senior girls left, the team that would remain (which included me) would be just . . . okay. It's not that the rest of us weren't talented, but while we wore the Life is Good "Softball is Life . . . the Rest is Just Details" T-shirts, we did not embody the mentality.

Even though I wasn't one of our team's all-stars, it didn't really matter because I *was* a member of the starting roster. As such, I enjoyed the privilege of walking the halls of my high school with the swagger of a varsity athlete. Our school didn't do letterman jackets, but sometimes on game days (when we would wear pajamas or pigtails for "tEaM sPiRiT"), the guys on the varsity baseball team would say hi to me. That felt pretty neat, considering I would not normally be afforded those types of elite-level pleasantries.

These sort of ego-stroking intangibles made the grueling two-and-a-half-hour after-school and Saturday practices seem like less of a burden and more of a pay-to-play kind of scenario. If I wanted to enjoy the perks of rising above my high school social class for one sports season per year, I'd have to endure some long-winded nagging from Coach Leslie about how screaming "G-DOUBLE O-D-E-Y-E GOOD EYE GOOD EYE GOOD EYE!" from the bench was crucial for ensuring victory. Or how I was "too focused" on "getting a tan" during our Saturday morning practices, which was nearly impossible given that I was always wearing fifteen pounds of catching equipment in order to become a sweaty human backstop.

Believe me, I've heard every justification for why coaches need to be tough on their athletes to help bring out the best in them. But even as high school kids, I think we all knew that's a bunch of, to borrow a phrase from our current president at the time of writing this, *malarkey.*

Fear-based leadership does nothing but churn out a hoard of obedient robot humans, who when given the chance to think and act for themselves for the first time won't have the internal compass to make thoughtful choices and will, instead, leap at the chance to be reckless. This is how we get dangerous outcomes spurred on by misinformation campaigns and deranged school board meetings over public-safety measures. When people are led by fear, there can only be negative outcomes.

For my part of this toxic dynamic, I'd like to present Exhibit A.

Just as our preseason was winding down during my junior year and tensions surrounding the starting lineup were running high, a few of the seniors on our team decided it would be a good idea for some of us girls to get together for a team-bonding night. To decode for those who are unfamiliar, team bonding can either mean "ordering an obscene amount of pizza from Papa Gino's and eating it while we burn mix CDs" or "Let's all go to Irene's house while her parents are away and drink Smirnoff Ice and share clove cigarettes." On this occasion, it was the clove cigarette version. While an intense fear of getting caught had caused me to weasel my way out of any such alcohol-infused scenario up until this point, I agreed to attend.

Due to intense Catholic guilt, I had spent most of my high school career with my flag firmly planted at the summit of Sober Virgin Mountain and did my best to avoid any parties where drinking might be involved. It wasn't that I didn't *want* to drink; it's just that I was worried I would be so wracked with guilt over my **SINS** that I would accidentally confess the whole affair to my mom, thus getting the entire softball team into the kind of deep, deep trouble that makes your parents say they're "not mad, just disappointed."

But on this night in April 2002, I said an impassioned "Screw you" to my moral compass and decided to try my hand at being *not* good for once. I accepted the invitation to drink malted alcoholic beverages with the rest of my upperclassmen teammates and felt like a 100 percent Grade-A Badass.

After pseudo-lying[2] to my parents about the goings-on of the evening, I pulled up at Irene's house in my oversized

2. I think these kinds of discretions fall under the heading of Lies of Omission, and even now as a parent I still think they're a pretty good flex. "But I didn't tell you there *wouldn't* be drinking!"

white Buick Century (which was sporting a gigantic dent in the rear fender, thanks to my five-star teenage driving skills) and parked among the long line of other hand-me-down and borrowed vehicles driven by my teammates. Armed with my contributions to our night of team bonding (a family-size bag of salt and vinegar potato chips and a two-liter bottle of Sprite), I sauntered up to the front door, ready to pass through this symbolic threshold into what I thought was true teenagerdom.

What I saw when I entered Irene's basement rec room was a scene not at all dissimilar to one found in every bad high school romantic comedy starring Freddie Prinze Jr. and a female protagonist whose *gag* glasses make her a social pariah. The boys' baseball team had already shown up with enough six packs of translucent alcoholic beverages to take out an entire sorority, and everyone was being careful to pour said translucent alcohol into red Solo cups so we wouldn't look conspicuous *at all* in case a grown-up walked in. I knew we weren't expecting Irene's parents because they were out of town taking her younger brother to visit a few colleges in Pennsylvania, but when the most exciting thing in your town is the fully costumed sunrise Revolutionary War reenactment each year, the police tend to be called whenever three or more high schoolers congregate in any one location.

I put my chips and soda down next to a charcuterie plate[3] and stowed my sleeping bag behind the couch. Most of my

3. Tostitos Scoops and Twizzlers.

friends on the team had already helped themselves to a Mike's Hard Lemonade or two, so I hurried to catch up, nonchalantly grabbing a Smirnoff Ice from the cooler. I made a bold attempt at asking for a bottle opener, before one of the guys from the baseball team leaned over and casually twisted the top off for me. Served me right for pretending I knew what I was doing. My goody-goody reputation was leeching from my pores, much like the water that was seeping out of the bottom of the cooler and soaking into Irene's carpet. But unlike the wet carpet, which would go completely unnoticed until Irene's parents returned from their trip, I was sure everyone at the party noticed how desperately I was trying to pretend like I belonged.

The rest of the evening was a potpourri of drinking games and Truth or Dare, with brief interregnums allotted for Dorito-eating and watching and rewatching the best scenes from *I Know What You Did Last Summer.* I drank and ate. And then because everyone else was doing it, I drank some more.

"I DON'T EVEN FEEL DRUNK!" I'd occasionally yell in someone's ear. And they would say, "You're yelling, Kelly," and I would say, "Whaaaaaat???" and suddenly one of my ankles would just stop working and I'd lose my balance for some reason.

The next morning, those of us who'd stayed the night, sprawled on couches and love seats in Irene's basement, pried open our crusty eyes and coughed cartoon-style clouds of halitosis breath at each other as we gathered our things to get dressed for our 10:00 a.m. practice. The basement was a fright—the boys had all left to make curfew the night before, leaving us to contend with the party shrapnel strewn everywhere. We halfheartedly tried to pick up as we simultaneously pulled on our sliding shorts and laced up our cleats. I accidentally put my sliding shorts on backwards, which was way more *hilarious* than it should've been, and I rolled back onto the floor giggling until one of the older girls told me to get myself together and help take bags of empty bottles to the trash can. I rolled back up onto my feet and obliged, suddenly feeling less giggly and slightly more like my stomach had turned into a ball of rotten death garbage on the inside.

With nothing available for breakfast besides leftover tortilla chips, we piled into cars and drove to Dunkin' Donuts for greasy breakfast sandwiches and Coffee Coolattas en route to practice. If you haven't had the pleasure of pouring a whipped iced coffee beverage on top of an "unsettled" stomach, you, my child, have been blessed beyond measure, because when those tiny ice crystals met the leftover Twizzlers, salsa, and Smirnoff Ice in my stomach, my insides made a sound like a Demogorgon in heat. Compound that with riding in the backseat of a seventeen-year-old driver's Honda Civic and you've got a recipe for blown chunks waiting to happen.

With absolutely no self-awareness and all the puffed-up confidence in the world, the rest of the team and I arrived at the field several minutes after warm-ups were scheduled to start, bearing an eerie resemblance to Walter Matthau on his first day coaching the Bad News Bears. I was still holding fast to my assertion that I had *not* gotten drunk the night before (because I would *never)* and had convinced myself

I was coming down with some kind of stomach bug out of absolutely nowhere.

At the very same moment that the contents of my stomach began organizing a coup, our team captains started leading us in our usual ~~death march~~ warmup jog around the outfield. My cleats felt like they weighed eighteen pounds each and my head was throbbing. But the really weird part was that everyone around me looked like they were experiencing something similar. *Maybe we're all coming down with the same stomach bug,* I thought. *I don't remember anyone writing their name on the red Solo cups last night. We were probably sharing germy drinks all night! Idiots!*

When this story replays in my head as a grainy PSA against teenage binge drinking, this is where the narrator's voice booms over sepia-toned B-roll footage of our tortured warm-up jog: *But they weren't sharing germy drinks. No—not at all. They were sharing in a consequence as old as time: the hangover.*

Sensing that something was most definitely amiss (like our collective inability to run one lap around the outfield without dry heaving), Coach Leslie called our team over to the infield with one of her trademark ear-piercing whistles and began what can only be described as the Longest and Loudest Lecture Ever Forced on Still-Slightly-Inebriated Ears. She didn't come right out and accuse us of imbibing, but boy, did she imply it. For like twenty-five minutes (or 115 hours, I'm not sure which), she insinuated it and then she alluded to it—hell, she even hinted at it once or twice. By the time she was done, we were all so dehydrated and exhausted, we would've copped to the whole thing if she'd offered us a cold, dark place to lie down.

Because she was so disgusted by our state, Coach Leslie said we'd be spending the remaining portion of practice running sprints. I think this was meant as a punishment, but in reality it was a lifesaving decision, mostly because we likely would have been concussed by any balls hit in our direction that day. But as we went to line up behind home plate to start sprints, Coach Leslie called me over to her. I assumed because of my previously unblemished reputation, I was going to be the one upperclassman who was exempt from running. Even if I had been the teensiest bit tipsy the night before, surely all the *other* times I'd *just said no* had to count for something. How much peer pressure could one teenage girl be expected to take?

"Go put your gear on," she said without looking at me.

"Do you want me to grab the pitchers to throw while everyone else runs?" I asked like a Bambi-eyed fool.

"No, you're all running."

I stood there dumbfounded, in part because my senses were still numbed from the night before, but also because this type of over-the-top punishment was usually reserved for, well, the movies. Surely she was not expecting me to run sprints in all my catcher's gear? I'd cop to the lapse in judgment that had me participating in underage drinking, but what exactly did she think I was going to learn by watching her kick me while I was down?

With Coach Leslie's eyes burning a hole in me, I stood there weighing my options.

a. Argue with my coach and most likely end up running anyway.
b. Quit softball forever and give field hockey a go. I'd always been partial to kilts.
c. Silently weep as I strapped on fifteen pounds of catcher's equipment in eighty-degree heat and run until I couldn't feel my face.

I chose option C.

And it sucked. You thought maybe this was going to be the part where I rose above adversity and ran the fastest I'd ever run in my life? The part where I stood up to my coach because I realized that trying to make kids feel terrible for making a mistake is no way to lead? No. Sadly, this is the part where I cry malted alcohol tears under my catcher's helmet for a solid hour—oozing out my body's last bits of hydration and hope. Because Coach Leslie reminded us that if we were going to play on her team, it was going to be on her terms. We were going to be good little girls and make all the right choices and fit into the nice little boxes she had picked out for us. And if we didn't, well then, we didn't get to play anymore.

I'm not arguing that our coach shouldn't have been pissed at us; she had every right to be. She had every right to feel disappointed and call us out on our poor choices. But as someone who held power over us, our poor choices had given her an opportunity to show us how valuable empathetic and compassionate leadership could be. Instead she taught us that if you're going to make a questionable decision, do it in a way that you are not caught red-handed by someone who expects perfection—because they're not going to extend you one iota of grace or understanding.

After our torturous practice, I went home to lie on my couch and eat plain Ritz crackers until my stomach finally began to settle. I bristled at the thought of having to explain my state to my parents, knowing they'd be as upset, if not more so, than Coach once they learned all the details. I was going to be grounded until it was actually legal for me to drink; I could just feel it.

When I heard my mom's footsteps in the next room, I quickly rolled over to one side, pretending to be asleep, in a futile attempt at buying myself a couple more hours before the hammer came down. My heart stopped when I felt my mom sit down next to me on the couch and put her hand on my back.

"Not feeling so hot?" she asked, picking up the nearly empty container of Ritz, a hint of sarcasm in her voice.

"Not really," I winced, preparing myself for my second lecture of the day.

"Must've been a late night."

She stood, readjusting my blanket and giving me a gentle pat on the head, before walking out of the room.

I waited all day for my punishment, but it never came. My mom never said a single word to me about what had gone on at Irene's house, although I could tell from our interaction on the couch that she'd had a good idea of what type of shenanigans had taken place. Everything I knew about my mom told me that she was not okay with the decision I'd made to drink with my friends, and yet rather than dealing with me punitively, she'd covered me with a blanket and told me to rest up. She didn't try to put the fear of God in me or tell me how disappointed she was; she let the natural consequence of overindulging teach me all the lessons I needed and decided as a mother, and arguably the most important leader in my life, to extend me a little grace.

I try to follow this example as I fumble my way through parenting my own kids; turns out, it's one million times harder than I expected. When you're a parent, everything in you cries out to try and control your kids, to protect them, to make sure they do things right the first time to avoid consequences, but in doing this we rob them of the opportunity to learn from their own mistakes or, equally as important, to watch us model empathy. These days when I'm feeling the urge to flippantly dish out a punishment when one of my kids says something rude or leaves the freezer door open all night (thawing out my secret stash of *after-bedtime Breyers*—I cannot tell you how crazy this makes me), I try to take a beat and remember my mom and the Ritz crackers and that I learned something much more valuable from her without ever needing to be punished.

And I learned, and this part is really important, that when properly nursing a hangover, one needs something significantly greasier than Ritz crackers.

CHAPTER 10

Hope and Change

These days, eighteen-year-olds are way more up to date on current events than the generations before them. As an "elder millennial" myself, I will fully admit to having little to no idea what was going on in the world while I was growing up and only watching the news when it was

a. the only thing to watch in a waiting room,
b. on in the background at my grandparents' house, or
c. 9/11.

And that's about it.

I'm not proud about this privileged stance on consuming

the news, but it's important to note because I need you to know how wishy-washy I was about things that actually mattered back in the early aughts. If you had asked me about the status of the feud between former BFFs Nicole Richie and Paris Hilton, I could've given you every last detail. But did I have an opinion on the US invading Iraq or the propaganda surrounding Jessica Lynch's POW rescue?[1] Probably not. But if I did, it certainly would've just been a regurgitation of something I'd heard an adult say. Because it was a thousand times easier to repeat whatever my parents' or teachers' opinions were than to muster up the effort to make my own brain cells get together and conjure up a novel thought. And, for the most part, that seemed like a pretty good game plan. If I emulated things adults said, then the adults who said them, they'd like that! It would involve very little critical thinking on my part, and I would be reinforced by everyone believing I was acting like a grown-up. It was a positive feedback loop that rewarded me for taking the path of least resistance, which is just about as problematic as an echo chamber can get.

Of course, there was the occasional teacher in school who would push back on this and try to help me understand different ideologies, but for the most part, our curriculum was made up of learning about how great the US government was

---

1. According to NPR, Jessica Lynch, Lori Piestewa, and Shoshana Johnson were all injured during an attack on their Army convoy in 2003. Piestewa was injured and later died in an Iraqi civilian hospital. Lynch and Johnson were both wounded, taken captive, and later rescued by US Special Forces. Lynch, a white woman, was lauded as a hero who fought back against her attackers, while Piestewa, a member of the Hopi Nation, and Johnson, a Black woman, were given much less media coverage.

at rebuilding itself post-Reconstruction and reading *As I Lay Dying* by William Faulkner, which didn't exactly *scream* "hope and change." The vibe was more, "This is how we've always done it, so let's just keep doing it that way." So that's what I did. I defended what I thought to be true and worked very, very hard to stay within those parameters. And just so we're all on the same page, my parameters for what was acceptable were very narrow. Like borderline intolerant narrow. Like, if you didn't look like me, talk like me, and act like me, you were *different.* And not in a "let's embrace and celebrate our differences" way—in an "I think less of you" way. But, oh my gosh, don't worry; I hid this festering internal bias by being so, so, so, so nice. Like *so* nice, you guys. And because I was nice, I didn't see a problem. I didn't see a need to change my thoughts because I didn't recognize them as even existing inside my brain. I was a very nice young lady; everybody thought so.

And nice young ladies do as they're told. They obey their parents and listen to their teachers. They pay attention in church and steer clear of controversy. And they let their preoccupation with niceness get in the way of becoming thoughtful, compassionate human beings who don't balk at the idea of change.

But like, they always hold the door for people at the grocery store.

It's hard to pinpoint when exactly I first heard an argument against women holding positions of power. I'm sure it wasn't a singular occasion, but rather a collection of little occasion-lettes that skulked their way into the four corners of my mind and set up camp. So much so, that when Hillary Clinton was running her campaign during the Democratic primaries in 2008, I said the following to a coworker:

"I would never vote for a female president. What if she gets moody on her period?"

What if she gets moody on her period?

WHAT IF SHE GETS MOODY ON HER PERIOD?

I know with absolute certainty that this was not a thought that was birthed inside my head because I never experienced emotional PMS until I was much older. Yay, adult hormones! But this sentiment was definitely expressed by people in my life. Not mean people. Not he-man woman-hater people. Just regular people. And I internalized it. I let what other people thought become what I thought, without doing an ounce of thinking on my own.

I remember the moment those words escaped from my lips so vividly.

"What if she gets moody on her period?"

I was walking up the stairs at work with a much older coworker, and he stopped. We'd been having a very casual conversation about the upcoming election, so I was surprised by the look of shock on his face. Without mansplaining or chastisement,[2] he turned to me and asked if that was *really* what I thought.

Of course it was! Wasn't it? I mean, wasn't it what everybody thought?

---

2. Thankfully, someone cared enough about me to say something and challenge me to think more critically. Not only about politics, but about equity for all people.

I could read the room. I knew most people weren't thrilled with the idea of having a woman at the helm. And if most people thought that, then that was probably the right thing to think. I took a mental inventory of the women in my life in positions of authority and came up with nothing but negative adjectives: Pushy. Demanding. Bossy. Yeah, I was right to agree with everybody else. We were right to want a regular kind of man to be president. That's what we'd done for like 200 years, right? And so far, it had gone pretty great. No blemishes on our record whatsoever. I mean, yeah, like the whole Comstock Act thing, that was kind of a mess.[3] And yeah, not letting people of color and women vote for like a very long time, that was also not so hot. And true, the "War on Drugs" didn't turn out to be as altruistic as it claimed to be.

Hmmm. . . .

I thought a silly comment about Hillary Clinton's menstruation was totally harmless, but the truth was that I was actually helping to burn the house down from inside. I was a woman participating in casual misogyny; playing into the idea that it's way easier to keep women down if you make them believe they're a joke. And when you internalize that kind of thinking, it then comes as no surprise when you get paid less for doing the same work or get called "career-obsessed" when you unapologetically work full-time. But the real joke here is how much time we spend telling little girls they can grow up to

---

3. Essentially, the Comstock Act of 1873 made it a federal offense to distribute birth control and/or information about birth control across state lines, as it was considered "obscene and illicit."

be whatever they want, only to cut them off at the knees when they actually try to be that thing. We have to stop doing that! (Unless the thing she wants to be is the owner of an Escape Room franchise. We don't need any more of those.)

Of course, these days eighteen-year-olds already know all about this intersectional feminism stuff. Just like they know how to make thick, white sneakers go with bodycon dresses and the best ways to help end climate change.[4] And sure, we could leave it up to them to save the world, because honestly, I feel like Greta Thunberg has a pretty good handle on things, but instead I'd like to propose us older gals commit to championing each other with the same enthusiasm we see in the younger generation. No cap.

I'm really sorry I said "no cap" just then. It felt wrong coming out and I should've stopped myself. How about this? We strive to emulate Gen Z in their passion for equity and empowerment and other things that really matter, but promise not to tarnish all their hip slang by letting it come out of our millennial mouths?

That'd be da bomb.

4. Not to mention understanding how to propagate plants like it's absolutely no big deal. *How are they doing that?*

CHAPTER 11

Fenway Ambassador

When I was seventeen, I got a job working for my beloved Boston Red Sox. It was only my second "real" job; my first being a tennis racket restringer and soccer ball reinflater for a local sporting goods store, so this whole Red Sox gig was decidedly a step up, career-wise.

The weird part, I'll admit, is that I never technically applied for the job. But I'll get to that. First, a little necessary BoSox history.

Way back in 2002, John Henry and Tom Werner purchased the Red Sox from the historic Yawkey family for $380 million. This was a big deal in New England, because in the entire time the Yawkeys (or their trust) had owned the team, they had never won a World Series. For more than eighty years, the good men and women of Red Sox Nation had been robbed of tasting sweet October victory; but now there was a buzz around town that this new ownership group was going to bring a different approach and, with it, the hope of winning the final game of the season.

Like the winds of change moving in during that part in the beginning of *Mary Poppins,* when all those basic nannies get swept away and Mary herself swoops down from a cloud with her talking bird umbrella, the new front-office staff arrived in Kenmore Square. Many were transplants who had previously worked together in the San Diego Padres organization, one of whom, Dr. Charles Steinberg, had been heavily courted to come to Boston in order to bring the "friendly back to Fenway." In the years prior to the new ownership's arrival, the Sox had become slightly less family-oriented—kind of like Vegas before the nineties . . . and Vegas again now.[1]

Since my first trip to Fenway with my dad all those years ago, my infatuation with the Red Sox and baseball in general had only continued to blossom. I collected box scores and ripped pages out of *Sports Illustrated* to tape to my bedroom walls. Did my fandom ever reach unhealthy levels? Maybe. It's possible I wrote a letter to President Bill Clinton demanding that he make it legal for women to play in the major leagues (it

---

1. Why did Vegas ever try to be "for families"? Do they think parents want to spend $400 per night for a themed hotel so we can explain bachelor parties to children? For that kind of money, we will just take them to the Fort Wilderness Lodge and let them spend time with the equally-naked-but-more-animal Chip and Dale.

was never illegal[2]), and some might remember that I stole an entire box of All-Star Ballots and voted two thousand times for Nomar Garciaparra to make the 2002 All-Star Team, but that was so long ago, who can *really* say? The important thing for you to know is that baseball had gotten deep down into the Doris Kearns Goodwin of my soul.

Throughout high school, my friend Noah and I used to go to Red Sox games together almost weekly. Our parents would drop us off, sans cell phones, a few blocks from Kenmore Square, and we'd fork over cash for eight-dollar standing-room-only tickets or twelve-dollar bleacher seats—anything to get inside our beloved Fenway. Noah and I had been friends since the second grade, when our interest in trading baseball cards and avoiding the school cafeteria at lunchtime created the perfect Venn diagram for friendship. This is why it made perfect sense that when Noah responded to a want ad in the *Boston Globe* from the new Red Sox ownership and couldn't make it to the initial job interview, I would go in his place.

Before this, the idea of working for the Red Sox seemed about as attainable as getting a job at the Pentagon. It just wasn't a thing that happened to regular people. So when the team put out an ad, lifting New England's version of the Iron

2. In return, I received some 4 x 6 photos of Al Gore and the Clintons, which was an absolute thrill. But just for the sake of this conversation, let's pretend that the word "thrill" means "drag."

Curtain, thousands of people showed up to shoot their shot. All kinds of people. Like people who thought wearing a full Red Sox uniform to a job interview would be a good idea. It wasn't. It isn't. If you're not on the team, don't wear an athletic jersey in a professional setting—ever. This goes double for you, Lakers fans.

With no clue how mass job interviews worked, my friend Julia, who'd also applied, and I had decided to show up to the initial interview together, both agreeing to hold our expectations loosely. After all, we were still in high school, and the "experience" section of our resumes listed things like student council and JV ice hockey. But when you put us (conventionally attractive, white, teenage girls) in a meet-and-greet interview scenario, next to forty-eight-year-old dudes in literal baseball costumes, we came off looking like twin wunderkinds, thrusting us into the next round of the interview process. And the next. And the next. And the next.

Finally, after several weeks of herd thinning, Julia and I had advanced to the final interview. Only fifty of the original five thousand applicants were left to fight for the twenty-five available Fenway Ambassador positions in the public relations (PR) department. Had anyone had the foresight to film the entire process, it would've made a great reality series for ABC: *One team. Five thousand super fans. Only twenty-five will survive. It's ABC's* The Ambassador. *Mondays at eight/seven central.*

To exude an air of maturity and excellent decision-making skills for my final interview with the Red Sox front-office staff,

I wore a neon purple sleeveless turtleneck from Express and a denim skirt. I assume Diane Sawyer wore something similar to her first interview with CBS News. I also took the T, Boston's illustrious subway system, instead of letting my mother drive me in a car that *didn't* smell like pee and empty McDonald's bags. Both choices screamed, "I'm a terrible seventeen-year-old and have no idea what I'm doing!" but it was *my* job interview, and therefore I felt I should be free to sabotage it how I saw fit.

When I arrived, I was asked to take a seat in a dimly lit, prereception area with a prereceptionist (with strong security-guard energy) before I would be invited to walk up the single flight of stairs to the actual reception area, with the actual receptionist, where I would sit some more to wait for my interview to begin. As I waited, smoothing the invisible wrinkles in my above-the-knee denim skirt, I started to clam up, partially because my chunky, sleeveless turtleneck was made of wool and it was the middle of July, and partially because I couldn't understand how I'd made it this far in the interviewing process in the first place. Especially because, as you recall, I hadn't even *applied* for the job. I half expected to be called into the interview room, only to be confronted with a *Dateline*-style "gotcha" moment where the team owners read me the riot act about impersonating a job applicant. But before I had the chance to fully spiral, the phone rang and me and my tank-top turtleneck were told we could head upstairs.

The interview room was set up panel style. Four or five members of the interviewing team sat on one side of a wood-grain, oblong conference table, and me and my residual softball uniform tan lines sat on the other. Everyone was nice. They chuckled at my story about writing to President Clinton and *aww*-ed appropriately when I told them my dad used to whisper the 1967 Sox lineup in my ear when I was a baby to keep me from crying during our family's weekly trip to Mass. I left the interview feeling confident enough to have a slight spring in my Steve Madden slide-on sandals while I walked back to the T station.

The team from the Red Sox called my house later that week, and not embarrassingly at all, my parents gave them my high school boyfriend's home phone number (where I was hanging out watching the season-one finale of *American Idol*) so they could reach me in all my pre-cell-phone glory. Naturally, my parents then had to speed dial said boyfriend's home number to alert me that the call would be coming *before* anyone at the Red Sox dialed the number, lest they be greeted with a busy signal. It was an impressive act of telephone gymnastics, considering the lack of technology available in the early 2000s. My parents were so excited, and I was too, but also, Justin Guarini was about to perform, so I *was* kind of in the middle of something.

When "the call" came in, a voice told me they were putting me on speakerphone, presumably so everyone in the office could hear my teenage squealing once they told me I'd gotten the job. They thanked me for participating in the long interview process and reminded me again that there had been an extensive, qualified pool of applicants, expertly building the tension on the line with the same prowess as my beloved judges on *American Idol*. I nodded along, as if they could see me, always keeping one eye on the TV screen just in case Simon Cowell said something especially offensive. I have to assume this was also a tiny act of self-preservation, because even though I was dying to get this job, a small piece of me worried that I was going to mess it up and it was going to take away some of what made the Red Sox so special. There would be no more standing-room-only tickets or stealing ballot boxes. Once I could see how the sausage was made, would I ever want to eat another Fenway frank? There is something so sacred about baseball that, even as a seventeen-year-old, I was worried about ruining my connection with it.

But just as my mind was starting to drift into a *Field of Dreams* level of romanticizing, I heard someone on the line say that I'd been chosen to join the team. Not the *actual* team; I wouldn't be playing left field, but the part of the team that wore khakis and got to get Diet Cokes from the break room. And because I didn't know what to say, I did what I knew everyone wanted me to do, which was find an appropriately high frequency with which to express excitement and blubber something about dreams coming true and my dad being so excited and other similarly appropriate job-acceptance platitudes—all of which were pretty true. Especially the part about my dad. And then we said goodbye.

My adrenaline still pumping, I hung up the phone several times to be sure we were really disconnected and leaned back against the sectional in the basement rec room where my boyfriend and I had been watching TV.

"So?" he asked with all the depth and earnestness one can really hope for from a high school romantic entanglement.

Soooo, I think they picked the wrong person! I'm really not qualified to do this job, and now I'm wracked with imposter syndrome and feel terrified that I'm going to show up on my first day, and all the real adults involved are going to see me for what I really am. AN UNQUALIFIED CHILD!

That's what I should have said, but instead I said:

"I can't believe I missed Justin's first song!"

Which yes, was a huge disappointment, but equally disappointing was me letting what should've been a really proud moment get marred by fear and feelings of inadequacy. My struggles with obsessive-compulsive disorder had conditioned me to believe it was easier to keep myself safe if I planned for the worst, and it was a total rookie mistake to think that by anticipating things crashing and burning I could insulate myself from those things actually happening. Because, of course, things would go wrong.

Things can always go wrong, but, and I hate to admit this, because boy do I love ruminating and making neurotic mental preparations, it's come to my attention that never have I ever stopped something bad from happening because I spent a whole lot of time worrying about it. So far, all this kind of thinking has offered me is a lot of unnecessary grief and a surprising amount of gray hair for someone in her mid-thirties. The good news is, much like my witch hairs, I have begun to accept that some level of unwanted worry will continue to sprout in my life, but also like my witch hairs, there are things

I can do that will help those worries become less noticeable and not completely take over my head. It's like balayage for the brain, except instead of hair dye, it's therapy.

Although trying to feel in control by planning for the worst is a great coping skill if you're say, planning a spring picnic or a land war on Russia, it's significantly less awesome when you're trying to experience something that is fundamentally good, like getting your dream job.

Or basking in the silky smooth second performance of Justin Guarini.

CHAPTER 12

Being Wally

If you're into American history, my hometown of Lexington, Massachusetts is kind of a big deal. It's where the battles of the Revolutionary War began and where Paul Revere conducted his famous midnight ride. If you're less into American history, you might know Lexington as being the birthplace of Saturday Night Live darling Rachel Dratch and *Survivor: Africa* winner Ethan Zohn. It's a cozy little community, about forty minutes outside of Boston (twenty-five if you drive like a real Masshole). Its population of thirty thousand is made up of an amalgam of medical professionals, homegrown small-business owners, and hemp-wearing academics who have oozed in from Cambridge and the western part of the state.

Back when my dad was growing up there in the 1960s, Lexington was a blue-collar town with real people working real jobs so they could go home in the evening to kiss their real wives and eat real meals while they ignored their real kids and watched the local news on their real black-and-white TVs that were embedded inside pieces of thick, wooden furniture. But somewhere around the time local officials stopped sending DDT trucks out each summer to spray all the neighborhoods with toxic chemicals, the town started to lose some of its grit and began to transform into the bougie borough it is today—one that boasts both a championship high school mathematics program and a 98 percent graduation rate. And just so you can get a true sense of the academic temperature of the community, Tim Berners-Lee, the Brit who was knighted by the Queen of England for inventing the World Wide Web, sent his kids to Lexington High School.

By the time I was nearing my late teens, Lexington High was ranked as one of the top high schools in the state, and our town had become so myopically focused on its intelligence-based reputation that nearly everything else went by the wayside. Local retail shops closed their doors to make way for SAT tutoring centers and real estate offices designed to meet the relocation needs of the hordes of Silicon Valley transplants and other fancy-schmancy types. Our entire town was feeling the pressure to "keep up with the Joneses," and some of us just couldn't hang. Or didn't want to.

It was around this time that I started to become increasingly focused on moving away—like far, far away. A girl can only take so much talk of "safety schools"[1] and AP prep classes before her regular-level brain starts to malfunction. With the prospect of an out-of-state college still a couple of years off and my hours with the Red Sox cut significantly during the off-season months, I started by scouring the local paper for after-school jobs that would carry me out of our little New England town, where there wasn't much left to do besides drive to a neighboring town to see if their House of Pizza was any better than our House of Pizza.

I wasn't particularly picky about the work I'd do. I was hoping for something in retail, but quite honestly, I was so starved for entertainment that if the right hot dog cart had offered me an unpaid mustard-squirting internship, I think I would've snatched it right up. As it happened, a few high school friends of mine had found a fairly satisfying gig at a neighboring town's ice rink concession stand—satisfying in that cute boys from other towns played hockey there and bought Now and Laters from them, and it paid a whopping $6.50 an hour. Both of these, in my mind, were pretty good perks in the world of after-school, part-time work. I decided that I would try my luck in the food-service industry and applied to work the snack bar at the Burlington Ice Palace.

On a gray Saturday afternoon in November, my friend Julia and I crossed over town lines in her Jeep Grand Cherokee and drove to the Ice Palace to check it out. That is to say, we

1. What really sealed the deal for me was when someone called one of my "reach schools" their "backup college." Enough, Veronica. Not everyone can get a four on their AP history exam.

wanted to find out if we too could sell Now and Laters to cute, sweaty hockey players from around Middlesex County and, if so, just how cute *were* those sweaty hockey players? And what would our employee discount on Now and Laters be?

When we walked in the front door and onto the rubber skate-guard mats that covered the place, our senses were immediately overtaken by the smell of damp hockey gloves and Zamboni fluid comingling with the aroma of funnel cakes and chicken fingers (standard New England hockey rink stink). We went to look for whoever was in charge—presumably a middle-age, droopy-eyed, I-could-have-been-in-the-NHL-if-it-weren't-for-my-sixteen-concussions-looking manager whom we could *wow* with our Lexingtonian sophistication and wit. These personality traits would, of course, prove completely unnecessary, because as soon as we were able to prove that we had enough sense to work the Fry-O-Lator without losing an appendage, we were handed our W-9s on the spot.

I looked forward to my shifts at the Ice Palace.[2] The Fry-O-Lator was the biggest piece of machinery my callus-free hands had ever operated, and I really liked pushing the buttons on the cash register. It was basically me as a kid, playing restaurant all over again—except I was *actually* working in a restaurant. If you could call a place that doesn't even have an oven or a menu a restaurant.

One particularly slow Sunday at the rink, I saw on the

2. Truly the biggest misnomer I've ever come across. If this place was an Ice "Palace," then Elsa was a much bigger badass than we all gave her credit for.

schedule that an assistant manager I hadn't met yet would be supervising my shift. Some guy named Geoff. I assumed that he would be another middle-age, concussiony-looking guy with *Bruh*-energy, to whom I would pay absolutely no mind unless I needed him to unclog a grease ball from the Fry-O-Lator's internal mechanism. I was going about my preshift tasks, which consisted mostly of turning on appliances and making sure our condiment bottles were sufficiently almost empty, when the new assistant manager guy walked in. He wasn't another middle-age, concussiony-looking *Bruh* at all. He was a young, muscley-looking *Bruh* with blindingly white teeth and a way-too-tight Abercrombie & Fitch polo shirt. So obviously, I immediately T9 texted my friend Julia that she *had* to drive over to the rink and look at the cute boy I found—and I hadn't even had to use my Now and Laters discount as bait!

Apparently, there was something about the way I heated up a soft pretzel that Geoff liked. After a couple of flirty shifts, we ended up dating, and, with my goal of meeting a cute boy met, I quit my job at the Ice Palace. Our courtship, like most relationships that begin and end before you're twenty-one, was regrettable. Yes, Geoff bought me turkey subs from that good place I liked and let me pick movies, but like a lot of girls who date guys who don't treat them well, I'm pretty sure I only tolerated our relationship because I liked the idea of having a boyfriend. And the subs. I really did love those subs. Once it became clear that Geoff and I had a vastly different idea of what a healthy partnership looked like, I mustered up the courage to end our two-year relationship . . . over the phone. Because breaking up in person would be, like, *so sad*, you guys.

And I really was sad, I think. I cried, so I must have felt something. But I think what I mostly felt was relief. I could sense that our relationship was very unbalanced, and, more than that, I could see it in the eyes of the people around us. Specifically, a few of my Red Sox coworkers. Geoff and I were in the middle of our second year of dating when the 2004 baseball season started up again and my friends in the office had experienced a front-row seat to a lot of our melodrama.

The morning after my breakup call, I woke up feeling and looking very much like I'd been visited by the Puffy Eye Fairy. And although I would've preferred to spend the day eating my postbreakup feelings like a rom-com stereotype, I needed to put on my Meg Ryan big-girl trousers and get ready for my shift at Fenway.

Because thirty minutes riding shotgun with a cold compress on my face sounded better than feeling obligated to wear sunglasses on an underground train, I accepted my mom's offer to drive me to the park instead of taking the T, as was my normal routine. As we made the winding trek down Storrow Drive, I stared in the visor mirror and attempted to will my face back to normal before having to face my adult co-workers. Nothing screams, "I'm the only teenager here!" like puffy, postbreakup eyes and a red nose. And as jade rollers would not enter my personal zeitgeist for another fifteen years, I dragged myself into work looking like Steve Buscemi's body double and prepared myself for ridicule.

I'd just plunked myself down in front of a computer, content to zone out for the duration of the workday, when my always-candid boss Ellen reminded me that our department was scheduled to pay a visit to a local Little League field on behalf of the team. It was an oppressively hot July day, and after my night of self-indulgent weeping, I couldn't muster up the energy to hide the look of pure disgust on my face.

"Also, you look like hell. You're going to have to be Wally."

Wally the Green Monster is the affable, large-headed mascot of the Boston Red Sox, so named for the park's Green Monster—the thirty-seven-foot wall in left field. The role, usually filled on game days by our professional mascot guy, Ron, was vacant on this scorching weekday morning because Ron had a real nine-to-five job so he could pay his bills. Ellen believed she was doing me a solid by hiding my disfigured mug behind the dense foam of the mascot head—and she was. Being only twenty-nine, she was still a card-carrying young person and knew I couldn't stand the idea of being seen by strangers in my current state. After I accepted her suggestion, a few of my coworkers and I piled into cars and headed to the Little League field—them in their Fenway Ambassador uniforms and me, still sniffling, in the bottom half of the Wally costume with the giant green head resting on my lap.

It was too hot to put the head on a moment before it was necessary, but it was also imperative, I was told, that I have it on before emerging from the car (so as to not scar any of the unsuspecting Little Leaguers). But no matter how much this point was drilled into me, the physics of the five-person sedan we were riding in did not suggest that this would be possible—not without using the shards of the memory of my broken relationship to slice open a makeshift sunroof in the top of the car. So when we arrived at the field and opened our doors to the sweltering July heat, I emerged butt-first and attempted to wiggle the giant foam head onto my body while bent at a sharp, ninety-degree angle. After forty-five terrifying seconds of boiling hot darkness, the head was on, and I pulled the rest of myself out of the car. Over the hum of the heat inside the giant head, I could hear the kids shouting for Wally.

This is how I'm going to die, I thought to myself.

It was only my first day of Single Lady freedom, and I was going to expire from heat stroke inside a Wally the Green Monster sarcophagus. Either that or I was going to be trampled to death by the two dozen tweens who were now jumping on top of me as I hobbled my way toward the event that was scheduled to last two whole excruciating hours.

What they don't tell you about being a mascot (well, there's a lot they don't tell you) is that once you are sealed inside your suit, there is no way to access any part of your real body. Sure, you can use your eyes to look out your mascot head's giant mouth, but other than that, your senses are generally immobilized until you take the suit off again. This means, if you are a twenty-year-old girl sweating and sniveling inside the dome of Wally the Green Monster's head, you have no way to wipe your tears or keep sweat from rolling into your eyeballs, creating an avalanche effect of salty facial moisture. So while on the outside I was gesticulating wildly alongside Red Sox great

Luis Tiant to celebrate the Little Leaguers of Boston proper, on the inside I was drowning in a flood of my own secretions.

Toward the end of the event, around the time I started seeing double due to emotional and physical dehydration, I overheard one of the kids who'd been jumping on me earlier say that he didn't think I was the "real" Wally. As I tried to figure out a way to flip him off despite having only four fingers on my mascot hand, I caught a glimpse of the look on his disappointed little face. I recognized it wasn't his fault I was having relationship drama or that it was hotter than the surface of the sun that day. He was just a kid who was excited to see his favorite team's mascot be silly and pass out T-shirts. Right then and there, I made an important decision. I realized I had the power to change my attitude, take the opportunity to become the best damn Wally these kids had ever seen, and do something truly selfless. I had the power to make other people's experiences change. It was something that hadn't occurred to me before, and I felt the gravity of the moment well up inside me, from my furry toes to my big, wobbly head.

So I took a deep breath, waved to the crowd, and marched myself right back to the car to blast the air-conditioning. Because I realized in that moment that that kid was right. I wasn't the real Wally. The real Wally would've conjured up some memorable Fenway magic in spite of the heat, giving of himself to bring joy to this group of children. But Budget Wally? She didn't come with that kind emotional fortitude preloaded. And she was going to take her "fifteen" to be selfish and go cry in the backseat of a Toyota Corolla.

CHAPTER 13

It's Been Eighty-Six Years

During my freshman year of college, I spent most of the month of October quarantined in Fenway Park during marathon five-hour American League Championship Series (ALCS) games against the New York Yankees. Because of my softball experience, I'd been asked earlier in the season if I'd be willing to act as one of the team's ball girls, which meant, in essence, that I would sit on the field during most of the team's home games (dressed in a full Red Sox uni) and field foul balls to give to fans. This special appointment had some really high highs, like on the rare occasion when I would make a great catch and end up on ESPN, and some really low lows, like when I got hit in the face by Ken Griffey Jr. and ended up on ESPN. But most importantly, it gave me literally the best seat in the house and access to the team's unlimited supply of Bazooka bubble gum.

During the Sox's playoff run in 2004, I was working at the park around thirty hours per week, while taking a full load of college classes. I was supremely exhausted and living on whatever sustenance I could scrounge up in the press dining room, which usually consisted of plates of squiggly dried salad topper things and soft-serve ice cream.[1] The postseason schedule was so chaotic, I was zipping back and forth to my college dorm for just long enough to attend the bare minimum of my class schedule, grab clean underwear, and update my AOL instant messenger "away" message: "At Fenway. Let's do this, boys! YANKEES SUCK!!!"

If you're unfamiliar, here's a brief recap of why these games were so important to us:

- **1918:** Red Sox win World Series.
- **1919:** After Babe Ruth sets the all-time home-run record, the Red Sox trade him to the Yankees, marking the beginning of one of the nastiest rivalries in sports history.
- **1920–2003:** A lot of good stuff *almost* happens, but never does.

1. In a tiny plastic baseball helmet, *obviously*.

- **2004:** Eighty-six years later, the Red Sox come back from being down three games to none to beat the Yankees in the ALCS and go to the World Series.

Now you're all caught up.

It's hard to put into words just how wrapped up in these games the city of Boston was. Of course, we all knew it was *just a game* and the world would keep spinning long after the box scores were printed, but there was something about wanting these victories—not just for us, but for our collective dads—that had six million pairs of eyes glued to the TV every night. Even on the nights when the team was on the road, my coworkers and I would pile into an empty luxury box at Fenway to scream at the TV together from slippery, corporate-style leather couches. Considering how flat my rear end was getting from all the hours I'd logged sitting on my rock-hard ball-girl stool, I was all too happy to spend some nights root-root-rooting for our home team from a slightly less dangerous and more comfortable seat.

Game 7 of the ALCS was one of those nights. After my classes had finished for the day, I'd grab my oversize hobo bag and board the free college shuttle to the Weston train station, hop on the commuter rail for a quick thirty-five-minute ride into the city, and walk the final five or six blocks from Kenmore Square to Fenway, all while using my French-tip acrylic nails to spin the dial on my iPod mini to my favorite Simpson sister song. And if that's not enough time period references for you, I can only assume I did all that while wearing low-rise bootcut flares and layered tank tops.

While the ALCS as a whole had been a wicked bad nail-biter,[2] in Game 7 the Sox got out to an early lead that they never relinquished. By the time the *Globe* and the *Herald* were working on their victory headlines for the following morning, my friends and I had all migrated to the top of the Green Monster wall in left field to catch a bird's-eye view of the postgame riots that erupted on Lansdowne Street. As we sipped warm beer from red Solo cups, we watched an absolute melee break out just thirty-seven feet below. People tipped over cars, fights broke out—it was lunacy erupting among a group of people who should've been weeping with joy. And while the whole scene was worthy of further anthropological exploration, I was dumb and young, so I said, "If I spat off the wall right now, how long do you think it would take before it hit the ground?"

World Series week rolled into Boston like an intoxicating cloud of bliss. The city was palpitating with a very specific type of excitement—men walked around with big, dopey grins, and women sported pink Pedro Martinez jerseys like they'd played every inning alongside the Cy Young Award winner. There were no bandwagon fans. Bostonians had been starved of a championship for so long that even the most casual fans were grandfathered into Super Fan status. It was the most Boston

2. *A wicked bad* _______: A participial phrase used to emphasize badness. Traditionally only observed in New England dialects.

the city had ever felt to me, and I was stoked to *take paht in the fahkin' pahty.*

Preparing to host the World Series was an all-hands-on-deck–type situation in the Red Sox front office. Everyone was working overtime on their overtime, and my boss and her bosses had candidly suggested my coworkers and I say goodbye to our families for the duration of the postseason. As our PR department prepared to take our posts on the night of Game 1 against the St. Louis Cardinals, Ellen, the same boss who'd benevolently suggested I play Wally the Green Monster, pulled me aside and whispered that some of the Sox executives would like a quick word with me in the conference room before the first pitch. *Awhaaaat?* For context, this would be like Taylor Swift asking to speak with a ticket taker before she started to perform anything from *The Vault* before a show at Madison Square Garden.

I plodded down the hall in my clay-caked sneakers (already in *full* uniform) to the part of the Red Sox front offices that had real offices with walls instead of workspaces and sharply pivoted into the conference room. It was an all-male cast of characters, all of whom were very much grown-ups in suits, while I stood there clutching my baseball glove, dressed like a ten-year-old on Halloween. After everyone said a very polite "hey, hi, hello," I glanced around cluelessly to see if anyone might let on as to why on earth I was standing in the middle of this room.

A few weeks before, a magazine of somewhat ill-repute had offered to do a feature story on me and my role as Kelly the

Ballgirl, and who could blame them; the story would basically write itself with that kind of wordplay. I'd eventually decided to turn the opportunity down after lengthy conversations with both my parents and superiors at the Red Sox. The whole thing had ultimately amounted to nothing and at this point was no more than a little blip on my radar. A blop, at the absolute most. Surely this meeting couldn't be about that.

Except that it was very much about that.

For the next five minutes I remember being encouraged by a room full of men to be careful about my personal choices and to avoid getting myself into any *trouble* by pulling a Lisa Bonet. The insinuation of course being that in one fell swoop, I could ruin my image by electing to do something (clutches pearls) untoward, like pose in *Playboy Magazin*e, a thought which had never *once* occurred to me, but was definitely not something I was interested in discussing in the middle of this episode of "Living Nightmare: Human Resources Edition."

Not knowing what else to do, I laughed nervously and then waved to Steven Tyler, who was walking by the room on his way to sing the national anthem. His hair looked exactly like I felt—frazzled, teased, and very much on edge. I wished more than anything that I could grab on to one of his sixty whimsical scarves and let him pull me away from the most uncomfortable interaction of my adult life. Turning back to the men in the room, I did the only thing I thought I could do to end the conversation and told them exactly what they wanted to hear. Then I got the hell out of there.

I rushed down the hall and through the red door that led

from the front offices to the top of the left-field grandstand. I'd just been assured by everyone that I was doing a great job, so why did I feel so strangely dirty, like I'd done something wrong? I reasoned that the men who'd blindsided me were just trying to do their jobs and maintain the Red Sox's pristine reputation, but

a. we owe Lisa Bonet so much, and
b. this type of "advice" still messes with my head today. Because I'm sitting here writing about this really upsetting experience and still somehow feeling like these grown men were "just looking out for me." And maybe the advice they were trying to give really *was* in my best interest, but a handful of adult males speaking to one teenage girl about what she should and should not do with her body—that's not cool. We're at work, gentlemen. Read the room.[3]

I stepped onto the red clay of the warning track just as our standard pregame music started blaring over the PA system. There wasn't a second to dwell on my disturbing circumstances because it was time to smile pretty while I sat a mere ninety-five feet from home plate and tried not to get hit in the face with a foul ball in front of thirty-five thousand people.

Again.

---

3. The Room being the entire female sect of the human race, who do not want this kind of unsolicited advice at their place of employment. Or anywhere.

CHAPTER 14

No Shoes, No Problem

After Game 2 of the World Series wrapped, a buzz started circulating among my coworkers that the team would be chartering a private jet to bring all of the employees along for the trip to St. Louis. This was one of the most fancy and exciting things I'd ever heard, and as such, I didn't think to wait until the rumors were verified before I started mentally preparing for exactly which of my going-out tops from Express would be best for the occasion.

While I was trying to decide if my sequined black cowl neck was haute enough, my friend and fellow ball attendant, Drew, interrupted my daydream to break the soul-crushing news that I would *not* be among the front-office staff invited on the private jet. Apparently, I'd just missed the number of hours to be considered full time, and that had excluded me from the invitation. Drew, who split his time between Boston and New York, was also narrowly disqualified. I was absolutely heartbroken. After sitting on the field for over fifty games that year, I was going to miss the two that mattered most *and* the opportunity to take a picture of myself on a private jet with my new digital camera.

But while I had already begun to accept defeat, Drew was hatching a plan.

"F@$! this."

Admittedly, "F@$! this" isn't actually a plan, but before the night was over, the two of us had committed to getting to the World Series together, no matter what.

Through some 2004-style Internet sleuthing (requiring the use of both the AltaVista and Ask Jeeves[1] search engines), Drew and I found two relatively affordable plane tickets to St. Louis. Unfortunately for us, with affordability came ungodly departure times; and extra unfortunately for us, those ungodly departure times were from an airport in New Hampshire, nearly two hours away. But we had made a pact, and neither one of us wanted to go down in history as "the one who bailed," so we bought the tickets and decided that our best chance to make such an early flight would be if Drew slept over in my college dorm room with me. It was fairly sound logic. My college dorm was closer to the airport

1. AKA Google's great-great-grandparents.

than the couch where Drew was crashing, and besides, now that I was unattached, I still had all my overnight guest passes available. What could go wrong? It was a totally perfect plan!

What we'd failed to account for in our totally perfect plan making was that both Drew and I were insanely exhausted from working a string of sixteen-hour, high-adrenaline days. Not to mention that between classes and late-night games, I was making the attempt to study for my midterm exams. I'm sure it was a surprise to absolutely nobody but us when, the next morning, we both slept right through our alarms, waking up in a frazzled frenzy at the exact moment our plane was boarding two hours away.

We'd missed our chance.

I slumped down on my bed defeated, an image of all my full-time friends clinking champagne glasses and dabbing their faces with warm, private jet towels running through my mind. The sun was just barely coming up outside and my body wasn't used to experiencing this level of intense disappointment before I'd eased it into the day with a nice dining-hall breakfast of cereal poured at a dangerously high speed from one of those clear dispenser thingies. But Drew wasn't so easily ruffled. He jumped up out of the vacant lower bunk where he'd been sleeping[2] and threw on his size twenty-six jeans. Drew moonlighted as Duff in a popular Guns N' Roses cover band when he wasn't shagging balls as a ball boy, and as such, his lithe, rocker frame required slim-fit Red Sox uniform pants.

---

2. You didn't think we'd been sleeping in the same bed, did you? We weren't *those* kinds of friends.

He reasoned that if we showed up at the airport with tickets in hand, there would have to be some way the airline would accommodate us, even if we had to beg, which I was absolutely not above doing. Especially when the alternative was to watch the games on the eighteen-inch TV in the common room of my all-girls dorm, while the rest of our friends experienced history firsthand. The decision made itself: We would race up I-93 north to the airport in Manchester, New Hampshire, and pray for a Red Sox fan to be working the ticket counter.

Like the McAllisters (minus Kevin) at Christmas, we sprinted through the airport terminal to plead with anyone at the airline who could help us find a way to get to St. Louis. We were in luck, the ticket agent told us; there were, in fact, two other flights leaving for St. Louis that morning. We'd have to be routed through Orlando International Airport, sending us on more of a checkmark-looking flight pattern than we would've liked, but we reasoned that a few extra hours in the air was a small price to pay. Drew and I exchanged our tickets and made our way to security with only a few minutes to spare until our new departure time.

In an effort to hurry things along, I reached across an FAA barrier to pass Drew his boarding pass, unknowingly triggering a sequence of events that required security officers to dramatically whisk us both out of line, frisk us aggressively, and send us back to the end of the security checkpoint[3] to

---

3. A very privileged you-broke-the-rules-at-an-airport experience, to be sure.

repeat the entire process all over again. As I set my overnight bag on the x-ray conveyor belt for a second time, I heard the PA announcer making the final boarding call for our flight. To use a baseball euphemism, we were batting .000 that day for getting on planes.

Eventually, Drew and I did finagle our way onto a plane bound for St. Louis, but not before realizing that not only did we not have a way to get to Busch Stadium once we landed, but we'd never *actually* confirmed that we had tickets for the game or a place to stay for the night. We just crossed our fingers as we made our way to thirty-five thousand feet and hoped our friends from work would help us figure something out once we found them at the stadium. As Drew and I sipped on cans of Deja Blue water and went back and forth about possible scenarios for getting ourselves into the game, a *very* thick Southern drawl from the row behind us said:

"Sounds like you two've gotten yourselves into a bit of a biiiiiind. I'd be happy to give y'all a lift."

If this were a *Choose Your Own Adventure* book, obviously you'd know not to choose the option that read *Get in a car with a strange adult man wearing bib overalls on an airplane? Turn to page 56.* Because that would surely lead directly to the end of your story. However, considering that Drew and I were desperate and, in fact, in a bit of a bind, we decided to accept his invitation.

To be fair, the man in bib overalls definitely did do us a solid, but as we sped along I-70, listening to him chatter rapid fire on several different cell phones about the game, I couldn't help but feel like this *solid* had one or two more red flags than I would prefer.

"He's a bookie," Drew silently mouthed to me, before asking our new friend to pull over at the next corner so we could meet our friends with employee passes.

"How much you think they would want for one of them backstage passes?" Our new friend asked, greasily.

"Sorry, they're nontransferable!" I stammered, real cool-like, and squirmed out of my seatbelt in the backseat. "Thanks for the ride, si—" but before I could finish, the overalled man was peeling away, talking loudly again on one of his flip phones.

Slightly unnerved that I'd mistaken bookie energy for Southern hospitality, I hustled with Drew through the crowd to meet up with our friends and make one last-ditch effort to find a way to get into the stadium to watch the game. With only a few minutes before the scheduled first pitch, our hope of getting to watch the Sox play in person was beginning to feel like a pipe dream.

What happened next can only be described as a World Series miracle.

Amid the chaos of ticketing more than one hundred full-time Red Sox employees, the Cardinals ticket office had accidentally allotted two[4] too many seats for the group. There were tickets for us! Me and Drew! Now this might not seem like a big enough deal to earn the label "miracle," but two

4. Drew + Me = TWO!

mysterious empty seats during a World Series game—that just doesn't happen. To celebrate, Drew and I bought a couple o twenty-four-ounce Busch beers and cheered the Red Sox to Game 3 victory.

The next day, after spending the night crashed in friend hotel rooms, we woke up to prepare for what could be tl final game of the 2004 season. If the Red Sox won Game they would sweep the St. Louis Cardinals and win their fi World Series in eighty-six years. It was an improbable outco to an unbelievable season, and *it was all happening.* The t magic tickets from the night before were still available w we arrived at the stadium before game time. From our s in section 255, we watched the Sox take an early 3-0 lead would never relinquish and covered our faces in disbelief v Keith Foulke shovel-passed the ball to Doug Mientkiewic the final out of the Series.

The entire Red Sox staff rushed the field like the c fans we'd watched only a week before on Lansdowne S and to our surprise, the Cardinals security staff waved u on through. Meanwhile, instead of immediately filing the stadium broken and dejected, the remaining for thousand Cardinals fans in attendance that night sta their seats and gave the Red Sox a standing ovation, ad the emotional hysterics I had worked myself into. I w bing happy tears and high-fiving anyone who looke direction when our catcher, Jason Varitek, the same g was still living in perpetuity all over the walls of my b at my parents' house, came over and gave me a huge

did Johnny Damon and Gabe Kapler, and finally, and most memorably, David Ortiz. Number 34. Big Papi. The future Hall of Famer lifted me and my runny mascara off the ground in a giant bear hug and yelled, "Girl, why are you crying? We just won the World Series!"

Somewhere amidst all the festivities, I caught up with Drew on the pitcher's mound, and in a sobering moment, we reminded each other that neither of us had a return plane ticket home to Boston. The rest of the Red Sox staff and players would be boarding their private jets in a couple of hours, and with nowhere to stay and no return flights available until the next morning, the best we could figure, we were about to spend the night sleeping on the floor of the St. Louis airport. A Debbie Downer moment, if ever there was one.

When all the players and staff eventually filed out of Busch Stadium in a mass exodus, Drew and I were separated. I grabbed a cab to the airport with a nice guy from our office named Wes, an MIT grad who had joined the Sox staff the year before, and we exchanged tales from the last two days. I shared the story of how Drew and I finagled our way onto the trip, including the bit about how we had no way home and were planning on spending the night on the floor at the airport, until we could catch a flight the next morning.

"The hell you are!" Wes responded, with all the bravado

that a kid from MIT *should* be afforded. "Once we all get to the airport, you and Drew stick close."

The manifests for the two private jets included a list of the actual players and upper-level executives on one jet, and regular front-office staff on the other. As the head of Fenway Sports Management, Wes was regularly in charge of logistical goings-on around the office, so it seemed like no big deal for him to have a copy of both the flight manifests. Or for him to walk up and take the gate attendant's copies and insist he'd have an easier time checking people onto the flights because he knew everyone's name.

"There's not going to be an assigned seat for you guys, so you're going to have to squeeze in wherever you can find room," Wes said while he hurried Drew and I onto the jetway. The rule follower in me did not like this plan, but the chaotic and unplanned events of the last forty-eight hours had helped set a foundation for a realization that by giving up control and just letting things unfold, I didn't have to be afraid of things not going the way I predicted.

Drew and I made our way onto the plane as our friends and coworkers cheered and popped champagne. I was dying to continue the celebration, but the endorphin high I'd been riding for the past two days was slowly starting to wear off, and I could feel my body crying out for sleep. Just a quick nap. Not more than five, maybe ten minutes. Then I'd be back at it, whooping it up and celebrating with the best of them. I swear. I kicked off my shoes, balled up my gray hoodie to use as a pillow, and fell fast asleep until our plane touched down at Logan Airport in Boston.

It was just after sunrise when I walked barefoot down the steps of *my* private jet, in the cool October morning air, feeling like a bonafide World Series champion. In the last two days, I'd missed an embarrassing number of flights, traveled over 3,500 miles, eaten my weight in ballpark franks, and cried more happy tears than could fill one of those twenty-four-ounce Busch Stadium beer cups. I set my backpack down on the tarmac and powered on my cell phone to ask my mom to pick me up. I would need her help to drive back up to New Hampshire to retrieve my car from the airport, where Drew and I had abandoned it two days before.

When my mom's car pulled up, I waved and walked toward her, a huge smile on my face. She smiled back and returned my wave, rolling down her passenger-side window to ask the only question a mother could ask in that moment:

"Where the hell are your shoes?"

Part 2

The Growing-Up Part

It's My Body and I'll Cry (and Eat Chips) If I Want To

CHAPTER 15

Pinhead

Until I was twenty-three I was a totally blank canvas. Save for my regular got-these-done-at-Claire's lobe piercings, I had no cool place to stick earrings, no tattoos, and if you don't count the half dozen bottles of Sun-In I used in high school, my hair was pretty much still factory parts. I realize this isn't exactly unusual. Tons of people go their whole lives without getting inked or installing those cool ear-stretching gauges that always make me think of a tiny person hula-hooping inside an ear lobe. But the thing was, after I graduated from college I didn't want to be a plain person anymore. I wanted to be someone people noticed. Someone . . . edgy.

It had been only a few months since I had packed all my

possessions into my little red sedan and driven the 1200 miles from Boston to Nashville to finally start my real, grown-up life. Until then I had been living in Young Adult Purgatory (YAP). If you're not familiar, I define YAP as that time between graduating from high school or college and moving out on your own. For me, YAP looked like moving out of my college apartment and back in with my parents. Days were spent on their living room couch, filling out job applications on Monster.com while the *High School Musical* soundtrack, Rihanna, and Missy Higgins shuffled on my iTunes. It wasn't bad. No, it definitely wasn't "bad." I was insanely fortunate to have a place to land after graduation. I had free food, free Internet, and free friends, because no matter how thick your "I want to get out of here" vibe oozes, your family still has to be nice to you.

Three or four months into ~~my emotional spiral,~~ living with my parents, I stumbled across a craigslist ad for a position with a PR firm in Nashville. Remember, this was in 2008, back when craigslist was used for more than just massages or murders, so I clicked "reply" and sent over my resume.

Unlike my first job in PR with the Red Sox, the interview process with Achy Breaky PR[1] was, let's call it, sparse. Before you ask, yes, I know *now* this should've been a red flag, but at the time I was eager for my daily schedule to look like something other than

1. wake up,

---

1. This isn't the real name of the country music PR firm where I worked, but wouldn't it be great if it was? Say it out loud.

2. check LinkedIn,
3. check email,
4. check Indeed,
5. Pop-Tart,
6. refresh email,
7. check Monster,
8. Cheez-Its,
9. refresh email,
10. refresh Indeed,
11. refresh email,
12. Triscuits,
13. refresh Monster,
14. cry, and
15. refresh email.

I accepted a salary that I was fairly sure would *almost* cover Tennessee living expenses and started planning cute outfits to snag myself a country music boyfriend.[2]

Despite what I'd seen on both of Taylor Swift's album covers, very shortly after relocating to Nashville I realized the general vibe around town was not all cowboy boots and sundresses. I was acutely aware that my belted J.Crew dresses screamed *my mom bought me this!* and felt like a total butthead trying to fit in with my new coworkers, who listened to Widespread Panic and had Pink Floyd tattoos. It was becoming painfully obvious that if I wanted to truly pass through to

2. This is such good foreshadowing, you guys. You don't even know.

the other side of YAP, I needed to start carving out my own identity. It would start with a nose ring, which I was certain would immediately make me feel like the most original, hippest person on the planet—just like everyone else in my office.

Because I wanted my new look to say "I live on the edge" without *actually* living on the edge, I made sure to patronize one of the "clean" piercing places in town. Despite its pristine reputation, King of Spades Piercing & Tattoos could've benefited from a subtle spritz of Febreze, or maybe just a whisper of an open window. I strutted up to the very trendy woman at the front desk, who clearly exercised her right to use her employee discount at any time, noticing the white linoleum floors of this tattoo parlor looked more hospital-y than I'd imagined, but I took this to be a sign of overall sterility. A definite positive.

"I'm here to get my nose pierced," I told the Front Desk Lady.

Strangely, instead of indoctrinating me into the pierced-people's union by showing me the secret handshake or congratulating me, she merely slid a clipboard across the counter with explicit instructions to fill it out and not lie about anything.

What would I lie about? *I'm actually superallergic to nostril jewelry, but I'm not going to tell you because my secret dying wish is to bedazzle my corpse?*

Confused, but not deterred, I sat down and filled out all the forms truthfully and waited to be called back to one of the piercing rooms and become *transformed*. I imagined how life was going to change once I had this glittering nose jewelry.

Now, when people were describing me, instead of saying "that girl from Boston with short brown hair," they would say "that girl from Boston with short brown hair *and* a nose ring." It was going to change everything. I was going to be so relevant!

Front Desk Lady finally called my name and handed me off to my professional piercing artist. After clumsily collecting my clipboard and paperwork, I walked with my piercer back to one of several rooms that lined the side hallway of the building and was told to hop up on what was definitely a repurposed hospital table. Regret surged through my body. Regret and fear. And nausea. I still wanted the nose ring and all the privileges that would come along with having my cool factor bumped up by a million percent, but one look at all the metal tools and alcohol swabs sent *get-the-F-out-of-here* signals to my brain. It was similar to the feeling I get when I find a really good parking spot but it requires me to parallel park in front of a bunch of people brunching on a sidewalk patio. It's like, *I really want this, but if this goes horribly wrong, everyone is going to laugh at me while they drink mimosas.* And at least parallel parking fails don't come with the potential of a staph infection.

As a thin layer of sweat started to collect between the backs of my thighs and the vinyl tabletop, Piercing Guy took out a large handheld mirror and felt-tip pen and asked me where I wanted the ring to go. I stared directly back at him and answered, "My nose." I'd like to retroactively bless that man for electing not to do an over-the-top eye roll at me and simply selecting a place on my right nostril to make a tiny dot with his pen.

"Look good?" he asked, holding the mirror up to my face.

Oh no. I hated it. What if that was a mole? I would hate to have a mole there, right in my nose crease like an old, crusty booger. Didn't I once break up with a college boyfriend because of a weird nose freckle? And now here I was, about to pay someone to create that exact same look on my own face. *Somebody do something!* But as much as I wanted to stop the entire process, I knew there was no going back. If I left, not only would I *not* level up into the next evolution of my coolest self, but I couldn't bear the thought of the painfully cool Front Desk Lady seeing me walk back through the lobby totally unpierced. No, I was going through with it. I was going to pay this man to put a bright, sparkly mole on my nose, and then I was going to go get myself an M&M McFlurry as a treat.

As I held on to the edges of my upcycled hospital table, Piercing Guy clamped my nostril between some tongs and plunged the three-inch needle right on through my flesh. And it was done. He turned away and I just sat there, tongs hanging from my nose, while he grabbed the jewelry to replace the needle. It was one of those moments when I could feel the weight of a life decision pulsating through my body. Maybe it wasn't a big or important life decision, but I did suddenly have an acute sense of *Oh no, what's Dad gonna say?* Sure, I was old enough to live on my own, drink alcohol, and vote for the president, but as I sat on that table with tongs hanging from my nostrils, I wanted a *real* adult to hold my hand and tell me what I was doing was okay. And even though it was a really small thing in the grand scheme of my life, this nose ring was the first real decision I'd made on my own, and I was really hankering for some validation.

"All done," Piercing Guy said as he affixed the little diamond stud right *beside* the felt-tip pen mark. Cool. Now I had a small, faux blue mole *and* a nose diamond. Not exactly the look I was going for. I jumped down from the table, thanked Piercing Guy for allowing me to pay him money to stab something through my body, and walked back toward the front of the shop.

Before I reached the front counter, I caught a quick glimpse of myself in one of the hallway mirrors. Maybe this wasn't such an awful idea. Maybe I *did* instantly transform into a totally badass Nashville bi-otch. My shoulders started to relax as I rounded the corner. All I needed now was a little validation by the cool Front Desk Lady and I'd be on my way. If she could just briefly glance up and admire me like one might admire a dewy monarch butterfly newly emerged from its chrysalis, that would be more than enough. This nose ring was going to be the start of a brand-new me, and people were surely going to stand up and take notice.

I sashayed into the waiting room and slid my debit card across the desk.

This is it, I thought.

I could feel the chills bristling up the length of my arm as she reached for my card and opened her mouth to speak the words I hoped would affirm the first important choice of my independent adult life:

"You want your receipt?"

That's it? Did I want my receipt? I mean, yes, obviously I'll need it for my records, but where was my approval? My fanfare? How was this nose ring going to make me cool if no one told me I looked cool? That was the whole point!

It's been fifteen years and I still think about the Front Desk Lady a lot. How people we don't even know have the power to make us feel so many different ways about ourselves in a relatively short amount of time. Sure, it would've been nice for her to have told me I looked cooler than Lady Gaga circa the Grammy egg year, but I'm actually relieved that she didn't. Our exchange helped to show me how impactful seemingly insignificant encounters with strangers can be and laid the groundwork for helping me shape how I interact with the world.

It was also a helpful study in the importance of researching establishments that are going to mess with your face, because it wouldn't be long before I'd patronize a less clean location and pay for it with an infection that caused my eye to swell up to the size of a lacrosse ball.

So ultimately, two really strong takeaways here.

CHAPTER 16

Pontoon Tinder

I met Brian on a public dock just outside of Nashville in the spring of 2008. He was walking toward me down the pier with his hair pulled back in a loose ponytail, one golden eyebrow ring glistening in the sun, his general musician energy suggesting he probably was not going to be very nice to me. I had moved to Nashville only a month before and my best/only friend Kates had invited me along as her plus-one to a party barge birthday party with some of her country music–industry friends. In my mind, this meant a day on a thirty-foot, all-white, P. Diddy–style schooner with a toilet on board and, dare I dream, a signature cocktail. It would be a social event so bougie, it would catapult my place into the It Crowd of Nashville society and guarantee me the status of my new grown-up life in the South.

However, completely unbeknownst to me, a doe-eyed New Englander with no experience in hobnobbing whatsoever, "party barging" is a well-known Southernism for a daylong party consisting of nothing but potato chips, coolers of Miller Lite, and very loud country music—atop a flotilla of rented 1980s-edition pontoon boats. But I was new in town and dumb as rocks, so when our rusted-out dory pulled into the slip, I just smiled and acted like it wasn't at all a rookie mistake to wear my brand-new 3-inch wedges for this exact occasion.

While our group waited for the dock staff to gas up our pontoon, I did my best *new girl with effortless self-confidence* impression, while I casually switched my weight back and forth between my feet because my stupid new wedges were already pinching and I'd forgotten my emergency Old Navy flip-flops in the car. With everyone else paired off in conversations, I was left standing with that same handsome, yet vaguely *Boondock Saints*–looking guy I'd seen walking toward me earlier. He was scruffy and tall, with a bright-yellow bathing suit and Ray-Bans so dark I couldn't see his eyes. Totes impressive.

Be cool, Kelly. Beeeeee cool. Nobody needs to know your bathing suit cover-up is also jammies. It's fine. You're fine.

While our group of twenty-odd twentysomethings milled around with no iPhones to scroll, Kates continued introducing me to everyone. When we got around to Brian, I prepared my right hand for a very disinterested handshake, the kind you get from a four-year-old being forced to "meet" an adult. But to my surprise, his handshake was in that Goldilocks sweet spot of not too hard, not too soft. It was just right.

In hindsight, it was superweird that I was walking around meeting new friends with *handshakes,* but it was a different time. Fist bumps weren't a thing yet (not that I'd *ever* greet anyone with one of those), and there's nothing more awkward than waving to someone who's like two steps away from you, so I landed on the only other available option that wasn't air kisses, because those are exclusively reserved for Real Housewives.

"Y'all ready?" A scrawny, bronze-chested teenager called from the edge of the dock. He looked at the same time much too old for high school and much too young to be trusted with gasoline, but he stood in that way that only people who spend a lot of time around boats do, with one foot on the dock and one foot on the deck of the boat. You could just tell he knew his way around a buoy. Our crew clambered aboard, flip-flops flopping irreverently against the sun-bleached decks and coolers clanging against any available shin.

Brian and I ended up on the same boat. Not on purpose. Or at least, not on *my* purpose. It was my intention to spend most of the day on the top deck of the boat, working on my tan and sampling the various contents of the potato chip buffet. Specifically, all the Baked Lays varietals some thoughtful soul had been kind enough to provide. I always appreciated a good baked chip buffet at a social gathering. It allowed me to give off an air of *Oh my gosh, I eat whatever I want because I'm a very chill person who is confident in my body* while only consuming a relatively small amount of calories.

Our flotilla chugged its way toward "Party Cove," moving so slowly I don't think we even created a wake as we huffed through the water, polluting both the indigenous lake-dwelling wildlife and the ozone simultaneously. It reminded me of the time I went to camp at Community Boating in Boston and the sewer systems of the entire city backed up into the harbor. The surface of the water glittered that day with the scales of thousands and thousands of dead fish, and we were told by our teenage counselors that it was safe to go sailing but not to "put our hands in the water."

~

Staunchly in favor of laying a solid foundation for future sun damage, Kates and I set our sights on two unsuspecting bags of Baked Lays to drag up to the top roof deck with us. We shimmied up the steel ladder to our perch like a pair of millennial pirates—towels under one arm, bags of chips in another, rolled up copies of *Us Weekly* between our teeth.

"Avast, ye scurvy mateys! Who do ye believe wore it better?"

As we peeked over the top of the deck, we saw that a handful of our group had already staked their claim on this prime sunbathing real estate. Disappointed but not deterred, we forged ahead, spreading out our towels toward the back half of the deck and settling into one of the three available flattering positions in which to both sunbathe and eat. It was so crowded, it seemed that the most economical use of space would be to lie on our backs and pour some chips directly onto our stomachs, which wasn't gross because I was twenty-three and therefore obviously not wearing any sunscreen.

I assumed my favorite girl-in-bathing-suit-while-eating position (lying on back, propped up on elbows) to maximize perceived stomach flatness, poured half the bag of chips out onto my now-sweaty mid-region, and prepared to feast. As the first bite of salty, potatoey bliss passed through my lips, I heard a voice from the ladder shout, "*Ooooh,* so that's where all the chips went!" My head swiveled to see the scruffy, eyebrow-ringed guy from before climbing up onto the roof deck, making a beeline for me and my potato-chip stomach. In a maneuver only women will understand, I lengthened my body out in a way that defied all the rules of physical matter, because in that moment I could think of nothing more anxiety-inducing than a guy I'd just met seeing a chip stuck in one of my stomach rolls. In reality, what could've been a better litmus test for a future relationship than experiencing someone not bat an eyelash at the placement of food piled on top of my midsection? But in the moment, this is all I could think of:

He's not actually going to take my chips away from me, is he? I called these. I've claimed them! I will not resort to eating Fritos. Does he not realize I've dumped this bag out all over my body? He's going to be horrified when he gets over here and realizes my cellular matter is all over the chips he wants to—oh. Oh God, he's just eating them anyway. He's eating them off my stomach. If my stomach sweat has made any of these chips soggy, I'm going to die. I'm dying. This is what death feels like.

But I didn't die. And the chips were only like, 13 percent soggy, which isn't even that bad of a sog ratio for chips on a boat. So we pretended everything was normal and ate the whole, heaping pile together.

And two years later, we were married.

I don't want to give all the credit to the Frito-Lay corporation, but without them our union would not have been possible. Maybe your love story has a slightly more refined jumping-off point. Maybe you met your partner while sipping a plucky little Beaujolais in Paris or while you were both studying literature at the Sorbonne (fancy stuff only happens in France—I don't know if you knew this), but that wasn't our story. I've never been the kind of person who gets revved up by traditional romance. Rose petals, candles, and star naming[1] are all cool in the movies, but give me a guy who loves salty snacks and laughs at my dumb jokes, and I come completely undone.

We spend so much of our young adult lives learning incorrectly that love and relationships are supposed to look a certain way. That we should have figured out how to be the perfect version of ourselves before we fall in love by *this* certain time with *this* kind of person who checks *this* specific box. But what real love is, is evolving individually and as a couple and

1. This was such a flex in *A Walk to Remember,* but once a guy named a star after me in real life, and I swear I gagged.

growing into the best versions of yourselves together. Versions that embrace your past mistakes, become stronger as a result, and, if I've learned anything, I know that this part is true—vowing only to eat full-fat potato chips for as long as you both shall live.

CHAPTER 17

First Steps

As a good rule of thumb, I would caution anyone against accepting a job they found on the Internet that involves working out of someone's garage. I wouldn't say this rule is written in stone, but if you're the type of person who would prefer a nonmurder-y vibe at your job, it might be something to consider. Not that I ever got murdered at work—please don't hear me saying that. I did not. But I almost did, three or four different times while driving there.

I was working as a "magazine liaison" for a country music PR firm, making about twelve dollars an hour to call places like *People* magazine and *In Touch Weekly* to ~~beg~~ propose they feature one of our D-list clients in their publication. It wasn't especially enriching work, but I did get a full hour for lunch, and there was a good Panera nearby, so despite the fact that I was working out of a repurposed barn at the end of a dirt road, the whole operation seemed normal enough.

Normal enough, until one afternoon when I was on my way back from Panera and a shirtless man with long, stringy blond hair stepped out into the middle of the road in front of my moving car. All I can say is that he was *very* lucky I had not chosen that exact moment to glance down to adjust my chunky elastic belt after my midday bread bowl or I surely would've turned him into a human speed bump. I stomped on the brakes while Shirtless Guy continued waving his arms over his head with all the believability of a background actor credited as "Distressed Motorist #6." However, to his credit, he was standing beside a 1980-something Ford Thunderbird that *definitely* looked like it would break down fairly regularly.

"You okay?" I said to him through the window I had rolled down one-eighth of an inch. The other seven-eighths were there for my protection.

"Can you take me to a gas station to fill this up?" He clunked a red gas container[1] into my window and motioned like he was going to get into my car with me.

I'd like to thank the Lifetime channel and their brilliant staff of writers for helping me identify this roadside behavior as a potential threat. Without the countless hours I spent watching made-for-TV murder movies, I fully believe I could've

1. Which I assume was filled with two gallons of straight chloroform.

fallen victim to the roadside Shirtless Guy. Because although I'd been warned many times as a child to never get into a car with a stranger, no one ever addressed letting a stranger get in the car with me! Was I accidentally luring him into *my* clutches? I did have a bag of Twizzlers and a puppy in the backseat. Wait. No. This is getting really muddled. No matter *what* I had in the backseat of my car, it would not have given Shirtless Guy the right to get in my car, especially because I saw him on several other occasions trying to flag down other female drivers, waving that same empty, red gas container.

I know!

Like I said, be wary of Internet job postings. Or at least be ready to quit when they start to feel unsafe, which is what I did shortly after Shirtless Guy. But in truth, I'd started to tire of the PR game, partially because it didn't feel like a good fit, but mostly because I was realizing I wasn't very good at it. I spent most of my hours at work watching the clock and G-chatting with Kates, who sat one cubicle over. Occasionally I'd get lucky and land a magazine feature for one of our clients, but Samantha Jones I was not.[2]

Not being good at my job aside, I was feeling drawn toward something else. What was that something else? Oh, I had absolutely no idea, which led me to committing the cardinal sin of "young people in the workforce" and quitting a paying job before I had another one in place. With rent due. And a cell-phone bill for my BlackBerry that I no longer (and

2. I'm really more of a Miranda.

arguably never) needed to check work emails. The clock was ticking for me to find some work quickly. And because no part of me was feeling supereager to hear any iteration of "I told you so" from my parents, I started applying for every available job in Nashville.

Your company needs a CFO? Ever thought about hiring someone who got a C+ in college algebra to shake things up? I'm your girl.

You need someone to do mindless data entry from their couch? My Internet's a little spotty, but I'll probably do a mediocre job!

Your restaurant needs qualified servers? Have you considered hiring someone who has historically failed in the hospitality industry?

I was casting a wide net, but ideally I was hoping to find something where I could feel good about the work I was doing. I'd never worked in the nonprofit sector, and I wasn't what some might call "qualified," but I was holding out hope that I'd find a plucky little NPO willing to give a gal a chance and a reason to put on a sensible Ann Taylor blouse in the morning.

Fueled by LinkedIn and a prayer, I went on heaps of dead-end interviews, most of which ended in offers for unpaid internships or volunteer positions, which would have been supercool if it weren't for some of my own personal hang-ups, like "eating food" and "staying in my apartment." So selfish. After weeks of searching, I landed an interview for a teacher's assistant position at an inclusive preschool for children with disabilities[3] run by the United Way. The closest I'd ever come to being a teacher's assistant was the summer after my junior year of high school, when I worked as a camp counselor during a weeklong, half-day baseball camp, so I can't say that I could pinpoint exactly what part of my resume screamed "hire me." But I was grateful to even be considered for the position.

On the day of the interview, I showed up in my eagerest-beaver ensemble, and thanks to the good people of OfficeMax, holding several copies of my resume under my arm in a manila folder. I answered each of the director's questions with an increasingly embarrassed smile.

No, I didn't have CPR training.

No, I'd never worked with kids with disabilities before.

No, I wasn't familiar with implementing positive classroom behavior strategies.

But, BUT—I did live nearby, so that was . . . something.

Ultimately, I didn't get the teacher's assistant job (which was the right call re: qualifications), but the school did offer me a position as a "floater." A floater, if you're unfamiliar with the term, is someone who floats like a delicate butterfly, or a turd in a toilet, from classroom to classroom, supporting the real teachers when they need extra help or when someone needs to take lunch. You're basically a warm body to keep them in compliance with the state-mandated child-to-teacher ratios.

3. I want to pump the brakes for two seconds and address the terms *disability* and *special needs* because they are not interchangeable, and able-bodied individuals should always look to members of the disabled community to learn their preferences for what type of language they prefer (e.g., person-first or disability-first language). One blanket statement I do want to make is that to say someone "is special needs" is never appropriate.

And it was the freaking greatest.

To this day, I still maintain that floater was one of the best jobs I've ever had. Sure, in the hierarchy of school importance, it went like this:

1. Director
2. Assistant director
3. Teachers
4. Physical therapists, occupational therapists, speech therapists
5. Cafeteria manager
6. Assistant teachers
7. Changing tables
8. Me

But I didn't mind. I showed up every day from 8:30 a.m. to 5:30 p.m. and got paid to play with little kids.[4] But it wasn't just the playing on the playground or doing dramatic readings of *The Very Hungry Caterpillar*, it was watching their teachers use PECS (a picture system that allowed nonspeaking children to communicate by exchanging images instead of words) or seeing how modified tools could help kids with mobility challenges eat lunch with limited intervention. I was learning that the job of working with children with disabilities wasn't to do everything *for* them like some kind of martyr; rather, it was challenging and supporting them so

4. There was also another good Panera nearby, but that was just the cherry on top.

they could become as successful and independent as possible without us.

One of my favorite students was a little girl named Michaela. When I started working at the school, Michaela was two years old and just the sweetest thing, with this massive smile that would take up her entire face. Like all the other students in her class, she loved to play and read stories and swing on the swings. But unlike the other students, Michaela would often arrive at school in diapers weighed down with waste from the night before, not having been bathed in days. Her clothes were dirty and ill-fitting, her hair never combed.

Most mornings, I watched her teacher, Ms. Laurie, discreetly bathe her in the classroom sink and help her change into the extra clothes she kept hidden in a changing table drawer. Sometimes Michaela cried because changing her clothes could be challenging. Her medical condition caused hypertonia, or extremely rigid muscles, which meant that guiding her arms and legs into new clothing could be painful for her. And beyond just the physical pain, with no verbal language Michaela could rely only on tears or facial expressions to let her teachers know how she was feeling or what she needed. It was often hard for us to know if she was hungry or tired or in pain because she didn't have a way to express those different discomforts to us.

I worried about Michaela, the sweet little girl with the giant smile. Not because I was some great, able-bodied hero trying to "save" her, but because every kid should be given an opportunity and the tools to advocate for what they need, like clean clothes or a fresh diaper. Or even just the chance to say, "No, I hate that yellow shirt; put me in the blue one!" or "Fish sticks are disgusting!" From where I sat at the time, I felt fearful that Michaela was never going to learn to talk and would always be trapped in a world where no one understood her.

I was eventually fired from my job as a floater at the school. Like, superfired. Like, the director of the school told me to do one thing (not let my little sister who was visiting from out of town come in to work and volunteer), and I did the opposite (let my little sister who was visiting from out of town come in to work and volunteer). What a ridiculous flex to think I could get away with that! Don't you just hate the younger version of yourself, back when you thought you were invincible? Strike that. Don't hate her. Learn from her. But I digress. Because the thing was, before I was fired I had technically already quit. I'd put in my two weeks' notice because I'd made the decision to go back to graduate school to become a speech-language pathologist. Or a speech therapist. They're the exact same thing. When I'm trying to impress people, I say *speech-language pathologist* because I'm shallow like that, and *pathologist* sounds smarter.

I'd made this decision a few months earlier when I'd seen Michaela on one of the classroom carpets working with her speech therapist, Ms. Cyndi. On that particular day, Ms. Cyndi was teaching Michaela how to use a Big Mac—a giant red button with prerecorded words and phrases on it—to help Michaela communicate when she would like a turn with a blue ball. Michaela would press the button and it would say *ball*, and Ms. Cyndi would give Michaela a turn with the ball. And Michaela would absolutely light up. She would laugh and smile and play and then give the ball back to Ms. Cyndi to request another turn.

I don't want to say this was a lightbulb moment for me, because I'm 99 percent sure I was also thinking about the state of Jill and Bethany's friendship on *Real Housewives of New York*, but something about watching that therapy session set off a domino effect in my brain that helped me understand what effective communication really is and what my role could be in helping kids achieve it. Because it didn't matter if Michaela could speak; spoken language is just one of many ways kids can learn to communicate with the world. Whether it be through tools like a Big Mac, or another form of AAC,[5] or something else entirely—it doesn't matter, so long as kids are able to connect with the world and people around them.[6] Everyone should get to experience that sense of autonomy, not just those of us who look or act or communicate in a certain way.

It's clear to me now that what I desired most for Michaela is exactly the same thing I would go on to wish for my own children—a way to tell the world exactly what they want,

5. AAC: Augmentative or alternative communication includes all forms of communication other than oral speech.

6. As an able-bodied person, I can't speak directly to this issue. But as someone who made many rookie mistakes early in her career surrounding how I expected kids to communicate, I want to stress the importance of valuing communication in all its many forms.

how they want, without fear of being minimized or ignored because they don't fit inside a certain box. And that my role as a speech therapist, and eventually as a parent of a child who communicates in a nontraditional way, would never be to speak for anyone, but to get the world to listen.

Part 3

The Getting-Your-Act-Together Part

I'm Not a Regular Mom, I'm LIT (Really Going to Make Sure I Get This Parenting Stuff Right)

CHAPTER 18

Busytown

Brian and I were newly married and technically still under the umbrella of our "honeymoon period," which incidentally was covered by the much larger umbrella of "new parents phase," which was shrouded in the "holy crap, we have no idea what we're doing, but oopsies, we got pregnant" era. And we went through a bit of a rough patch. I guess it was more of a prolonged skid into financial disaster and emotional calamity. But "rough patch" sounds a lot cuter.

To start, things weren't exactly shaking out like we'd imagined when we first got engaged. Exhibit A: I was very much pregs at our wedding. It wasn't something we had planned; in fact, it was something we were actively trying to avoid. But when, as a couple, you've ping-ponged around a purity culture in which you try to avoid pregnancy by avoiding sex, that usually goes really, really well. So well, in fact, that one summer afternoon in 2009 while Brian was out on tour, I found myself sobbing in an urgent care clinic parking lot after a male doctor with absolutely no affect said "congratulations" regarding my unplanned pregnancy. Of course, *now* I know that having my oldest son Oliver would be one of the *very* best parts of my life, but at the time all I could think about was the fact that I was worried I had let everyone down. I wasn't concerned about whether I'd have appropriate medical care or about financially supporting my son once he was born, because in my bubble of privilege, I knew those things would be taken care of whether or not I was a disappointment.

I was just scared to death that people would look at me and see a girl who "got herself into trouble" and "trapped herself a husband." *Oh, the humiliation!* And so I sat frozen in my car outside of the urgent care clinic, squeezing the steering wheel and willing Brian to pick up his phone while out on tour a thousand miles away. "Pick up. Pick up. Pick up. Pick up. Pick up. Pick up. Pick up. Pick up. Pick up."

When he finally did pick up his phone, standing with his bandmates on the sidelines of a basketball game in St. Louis, Brian didn't miss a beat. I think he said something along the lines of, "It's faster than the timeline we planned, but to be totally honest with you, I'm pumped!" Typical Brian. Ever the optimist. Meanwhile, I'm spinning out of control faster than a plastic Spirograph stencil on a crappy piece of construction paper. Not because I didn't want to become a mom, but because, regardless of our family's and friends' reactions, I still carried a lot of shame from a lifetime of existing in a culture that stigmatized unmarried pregnant women.

It's true, I didn't feel "mom ready." I had lots of things I wanted to do first—like finish school and travel and watch a lot more uninterrupted reality TV. But I don't think you're ever really *ready* to be a parent. I have three elementary-school-age kids now, and sometimes I'm still like, "How am I the one in charge?" But in that moment, after I'd hung up with Brian and was sitting alone in my car, I felt like I was existing in one of those dreams where you're supposed to perform in a play, but you don't know any of your lines and are inexplicably in your underwear. Someone had called "Action!" from the wings, and I was just supposed to embody this role that I had no idea how to play—and had certainly not okayed the script.

But I did the only thing there was to do—I put my car in "drive" and went home to my empty apartment. Well, almost empty. I had volunteered to dogsit for a friend while she was out of town, so I went home and cried to somebody else's dog and scarfed an entire box of cereal. Strategizing how to break this news to my family was going to take all the sugar-fueled brain power Kellogg's had to offer.

First on the docket would be my brother Mark. In a family of white sheep, Mark was "eggshell." He had an inside-the-lip tattoo and routinely traveled alone in foreign countries on other continents. Our own family's version of unorthodox, Mark was the safest recipient for my first call. Only eighteen months my junior, Mark often felt like a big brother—in part because he stood at least eight inches taller than me, but mostly because he always carried himself with a cool confidence that said, "I don't need your approval," without wreaking of arrogance. He wasn't an all-star athlete or an honor-roll student, but people had always been drawn to him, so much so that when he entered high school two years after me, I immediately became "Mark Barons's sister."

Once I had Mark's blessing, I knew I'd have the confidence to call my mom. And then, once I'd mustered up all the strength musterable, my dad. Oh, the utter horror of having to admit to your father that you've had sex. Sure, I didn't *want* to discuss the subject with either of my parents, which was why it was very convenient that a much-older neighborhood kid had told me about the birds and the bees in the back of our family's Volvo station wagon when I was five. But discussing it with my dad was going to be a very special kind of hell. Maybe a baseball metaphor would soften the blow? I doubted it.

Although I'd always known he'd be supportive, Mark's enthusiastic "Congratulations!" over the phone was a massive relief. Enough so that I felt emboldened to call my mom to break the news. I repeated the information just as I'd shared it with Mark, only this time I couldn't hold back my tears.

As much as we all detest Zoom these days, I can't help but think it would've been nice to invite my entire family to a meeting and break the news to them all at once, with a kooky virtual background to soften the blow. In the end, Mom and I decided it would be best if both Brian and I shared the news with my dad in person, even if it meant we had to fly all the way to Boston.

And so we did.

The master plan was that Brian and I would sit down and tell my dad together as soon as we got to my parents' house after our flight. But as we sat in the backseat of my dad's pickup truck on the way home from the airport, Brian went off-book and asked my dad if he wanted to grab a beer, just the two of them. My mom shot me a nervous glance from the front seat, which I promptly returned with an I-have-no-idea-what-is-happening look, to which Brian responded with an I-got-this-don't-worry hand squeeze.

Because most life events in small towns happen inside the walls of the local Chili's Bar and Grill, my brother Mark also happened to be seated in the dining room when my dad and Brian sat down for their beer. And being wise to the whole pregnancy situation, Mark knew that the most brotherly thing he could do in this particular situation would be to text me a play-by-play of absolutely everything that happened:

"They're ordering."

"Brian's talking."

"Brian's still talking."

"Dad's head is in his hands."

"Dad's laughing."

"They're splitting an appetizer trio."

"Leaving. Dad has his arm around Brian."

"It's gonna B OK."

IT WAS GONNA B OK!

Now, did I actually believe my father was going to take my soon-to-be husband out behind our local Chili's Bar and Grill and snap his kneecaps like a couple of overcooked mozzarella sticks? No. But did I want my dad to resent my soon-to-be husband when he had to be the one to walk me down the aisle at our wedding? Also no. I just wanted everyone to keep their kneecaps *and* have the only uncomfortable thing about my wedding be the weird TMI situation during the wedding party toasts. And thanks to Chili's never-fail appetizer trio, I got my wish.

In case you're ever in this same boat, I'd like to present you with a list of things that are both superficial and totally great about being pregnant at your wedding[1]:

1. Your boobs will look spectacular.
2. You will not get drunk on champagne and forget the whole night.
3. You will feel zero pressure to work on your "wedding body" before your big day.

Overall, the wedding itself was a ten out of ten, loads of

1. I know people have all kinds of feelings about sex and when you should have it and when you shouldn't, and I'm definitely not the authority on telling you what to do with your body or what to teach your kids, but I'd like to suggest avoiding a shame-based approach. It doesn't work, and it leads to a lot of unhealthy practices and expectations.

fun, would highly recommend. The year following the wedding? Well, it had some highlights: I learned how to make a delicious three-bean chili, Brian started brewing pretty decent beer in our bathtub, and we took a lot of walks together—mostly to help me review flashcards for my anatomy and physiology class. For the most part, we just continued doing what we'd been doing while we were dating, but now with rings! Although mine were getting increasingly tighter by the day, thanks to both hormones and the two-for-one promotion our local frozen yogurt shop was running, exclusively for pregnant women.

Just after our first Christmas as a married couple, things started to unravel. Without warning, Brian's record label shut down.[2] In 2010 a band without a record label was essentially a ship without a rudder—if you imagine that, instead of being made of wood, the rudder was made of money. So what I'm saying is, there was no more money. No gravy train. No cashola. Brian was out of a job, and we had a baby coming. A baby that would need diapers and wipes and lots of teeny-tiny shoes for some reason. *How would we pay for all the shoes, Brian?* While I saw red, Brian saw an opportunity to branch off and start his own rock band. But with paying gigs few and far between (or never—there were never any paying gigs), Brian started working a commission-based, hourly job hocking

2. When we first met, Brian was a professional musician with a band and a record deal and everything! It was very cool, but I swear I wasn't a groupie. Well, I swear I wasn't *that* much of a groupie. But how many twenty-three-year-old girls that you know could resist a guy with a guitar? And a dreamy singing voice? Who, if you squinted a little bit in the right light, maybe looked a little bit like Keith Urban? Zero twenty-three-year-old girls, that's how many.

musical equipment for Guitar Center, and I wrote blurbs for a celebrity gossip website.

For me, a loud and proud reality TV junkie, this gig was half dream job, half soul-sucking torture. While I have spent a lot of time in therapy, I've never come to terms with the depths to which I'd sunk for that paycheck. Have you ever opened TMZ or Radar Online and thought, *What kind of monster would write headlines like "Teen Mom Cast Only Procreates to Secure New Contracts!"*? For the low, low price of $750 per month, that monster was me.

Of course, I should have been grateful for a job that paid, a roof over our heads, and food on the table, but I was a twenty-six-year-old white millennial, so instead I was laser-focused on how unfair and unfulfilling I felt life had become.

We can't even afford cable!

We have to quit our gym membership!

We have to work jobs we don't like that much!

And then the baby came. And everything was magnified 10,000-fold. The waking up ten times a night, the sore nipples, the red bottoms, the leaky diapers, and all of the other things made me feel like I was about to be buried under an avalanche of tedious moments. I felt mean and snippy and exhausted—like a dried-out husk of my former self. And I didn't really like her all that much. But then there was the baby, and I liked him a whole bunch.[3]

Every day we'd do the typical mom-and-first-baby things,

3. If you ever have the pleasure of meeting my son Oliver, the human exclamation point, you'll know what I mean.

like going to story time at the library, going to the park, sitting in front of the mirror and acting out the first ever late-night talk show hosted by a talking baby—just normal stuff. And at night, because Brian often worked second shift, we'd watch *The Busy World of Richard Scarry.* The swell of the show's theme song was our nightcap, cueing us to bid farewell to whatever the day held and fade into the world of Huckle Cat, Lowly Worm, and Bananas Gorilla. The show was broken into three short segments, punctuated at each break with a short song intended to teach some kind of life lesson—don't cross the street without a grown-up, fire is dangerous, eat your fiber—all set to a melodious earworm that would get stuck in our heads for weeks. I looked forward to our nightly viewing of Busytown as much, if not more, than Oliver. It was a happy place, where nobody's dad worked through bedtime and the moms never got angry and said "damn it" while they changed a diaper.

Even after things slowly started to improve for our family financially and Brian no longer had to work until long after Oliver was asleep, we'd still curl up together on the couch and check in with the Busytown gang every night. The show was our family's security blanket, reminding us that no matter how tough or tedious things got, we could come back to this place, this little oasis on our couch, and remember that everything that really mattered was right there—the mom, the dad, and the Huckle Cat, which was what Oliver insisted we call him back then.

To which we happily obliged because, as I mentioned before, we had no idea what we were doing.

CHAPTER 19

ETA

I remember Brian telling me once that he hated when anyone would text him, "ETA?" He said it made him feel stressed, like whoever was waiting for him at his destination was *already* pissed at him, even though he wasn't technically late yet. So because I care about him very, very much and would never, ever want to do anything to upset him, as his wife I very purposefully only text him things like

"Coming home anytime soon?"

"Thought you said you'd be home at 5 . . ."

"Where R U?"

Although it might present as the contrary, when I send those texts I'm never trying to be a bother. Or a nag. Or any one of the other *King of Queens* wife archetypes Hollywood loved in the early 2000s. In fact, I'd argue that "Where are you?" texts are the love letters of the digital age. If you'll just imagine that while wearing a corset and a hoop skirt I used a quill instead of a phone to compose those iMessages, suddenly the whole thing feels infinitely more Jane Austen.

Because when I send those texts, I'm not being a pain. I'm being vulnerable. I'm waving a white flag (probably more of a muted gray because I do not and will never separate my laundry). I'm admitting, "I need your help. I can't do this alone. And also, can you please grab some paper towels on your way home?" When I text ETA, what I really mean is Extra Togetherness Always. Because unlike when I'd slip a carefully worded note in the slats of some boy's locker in middle school or send a way-too-breezy Instant Message in my early dating life, an ETA text isn't sent to try to fool someone into liking a pretend, laid-back version of me. An ETA text is as real as it gets. But back when I returned to work a few months after giving birth to our second son, Archie, I had come to understand absolutely none of this.

Admittedly, our childcare plan for my return to work was not what you'd call airtight. We were operating under misguided assumptions that both Brian and I could work out of the house without any help, and we piece-mealed together a part-time schedule for me, during which Brian would work from home and keep both kids. And maybe do some light cleaning and laundry—possibly start dinner, but no pressure! In practice, I suppose the plan could've worked; it did have legs, but what neither Brian nor I took into account was . . . the children. Especially children of the still-in-diapers variety, who don't care one single iota if you are trying to work. It never crossed our minds that a three-year-old could look you dead in the eyes while you're in the middle of a conference call and ask, in their loudest voice, for you to wipe their butt. Or that an infant would spew regurgitated milk all over important contracts on the kitchen table/your desk and then smile about it—like an absolute monster.

No, sir. Those scenarios did not cross our grown adult minds. And even if our original plan *wasn't* exactly perfect, I was *only* working twenty hours a week. Surely it couldn't be *that* bad. So during my first week of work as a preschool speech therapist, while sitting on a three-legged stool in a closet, hooked up to a hydraulic pump that was milking me like a dairy cow, I felt a slight twinge of annoyance when my phone buzzed with an SOS text from Brian.

"When will you be home? Archie didn't nap," he nagged me via a gray text bubble.

When would I be home? I'd only been gone long enough to fill my milk ducts a single time. Was he really already texting me about one crummy nap?

"Normal time," I typed back aggressively, my nipples stretching in and out rhythmically.

I mean, honestly, how hard could a couple of days at home with his kids possibly be? I did it all the time. In fact, I'd done it almost every single day for the past three years. And I'd cleaned and done laundry and made dinner every night—not that I'm comparing! How dare he pester me about something so simple? My frustration with Brian was causing my body temperature to rise to a point where I was concerned about my milk curdling, so I unsuctioned my breasts from their silicone shields and packed the four hundred different pieces of my breast pump into its Sleek 'n' Discreet Tote Bag.

I was so put out. So frustrated. So annoyed that Brian wouldn't be able to hold down the fort while I had something that was *mine* for a few hours a week. The whole thing felt very outdated and unfair.

My phone rang while I was on my way home from work at the "regular time" later that day. It was Brian.

"Hello?" I said, while rolling my eyes all the way to the back of my head. What could he possibly need? I was thirty-eight minutes from the front door.

I could hear Archie, my five-month-old, wailing in the background. He was cutting teeth, and even without tiny hunks of dentin puncturing the undersides of his gums, he generally presented with the disposition of a disgruntled eighty-three-year-old man being forced to wait too long for his Arnold Palmer.

"Are you on your way?" Brian's voice muffled by the screams.

"Brian," I sighed (loudly and intentionally), "I told you when I'd be home. I'm coming as fast as I can."

And then he started to cry. Brian, not Archie. Archie was

already crying. At this point, the only one not crying in the house was our three-year-old, Oliver, who was undoubtedly playing a rock 'n' roll version of *Baa Baa Black Sheep* on a Fisher-Price guitar in his bedroom. "I can't do this, Kel. I can't do this with the both of them here."

The same rage from before started to bubble in my stomach, and I opened my mouth to lay into Brian about not being able to take care of our kids on his own, when I caught myself.[1] Something felt different about this phone call. Brian didn't sound annoyed or resentful; he sounded like me. He sounded overwhelmed. I realized that Brian's calls and texts wondering when I would be home were not, as I thought, rooted in him wanting me to be in charge of the kids; they were coming from a vulnerable place where he felt safe enough to tell me he needed help, because there is no human being alive on planet earth who can fire on all cylinders while working from home with small children. It's impossible; it cannot be done. At least not well. There may be some higher-level parents out there who have unlocked some secret we don't know down here in the lowly Bandas house, but it's been our experience that working from home with children might be just about the hardest career move there is.

On my thirty-eight-minute drive home that day, Brian and I talked through some alternative scenarios for our kids while I was at work. We didn't move any mountains in that one phone call, but what I gained from our conversation was

1. Maybe I did give him a little bit of a hard time first. But who can remember these things?

a beginning of the understanding that an ETA text, no matter who sends it, means a hell of a lot more than "Where are you?"

It means "I trust you."

And also, can you please pick up some paper towels?

CHAPTER 20

The Things We Carried

I love checkout aisle magazines. You know the kinds I'm talking about—the ones that do their best to remind me and my unwashed hair that celebrities are *just like us,* while simultaneously making my life seem cheap, boring, and very untoned. It's all the soul-destroying content you could ever want, for $3.95.

And while there's a part of me that loves the voyeurism these rags afford, my all-time favorite "articles" are the ones where they take a celebrity's Fendi[1] handbag and dump it out

1. Full disclosure, I just clicked over to Nordstrom.com and did a search for their most expensive purses, because I literally could not think of a fancy enough brand to list here.

to reveal a cornucopia of ultraexpensive beauty products and exactly one pseudo-embarrassing item, like a worn-out nail file or tube of *gasp* regular-brand lip balm.

Eek! You caught me. I use Carmex. I'm such a dork!

Listen, if celebrities were anything at all like us, their purse dumps would reveal a lot more about them than these types of articles are willing to divulge. Because if I were to grab whichever Target purse was closest to me right now and dump it out for the world to see, well, there'd be no need for this book because you'd already know everything there is to know about me. The contents of a person's purse or diaper bag (or over-the-shoulder messenger bag if it's 1999) are the true marks of their character, and in the spirit of *really* getting to know each other on a deep level, I'd like to present mine to you.

1. A Rumpled-Up Feminine Hygiene Product, Still (Sort of) in the Wrapper

   I have reached the point in my menstruation maturity at which I am no longer willing to roll the dice with period protection. Not only am I forced to constantly monitor my uterine lining for signs that my monthly visitor might be on her way,[2] but I'm also expected to just trust that some random lady at the YMCA might have my brand of underwear Band-Aid? Not happening.

   It would be gross negligence on my part to take my

2. Is it coming? Where is it? Is it late? Am I pregnant? Oh, okay. I got it. Wait, was that it? Where did it go?

old, but unused tampons/menstrual cups *out* of my bag. Because, quite frankly, I would rather use a tampon covered in graham cracker crumbs and melted ChapStick than tempt fate by throwing it out—which would be the equivalent of spitting into the wind, if your spit was made of old cells, which it is, but you get my point.

2. A Ziploc Bag of Stale Goldfish

   Kids are hungry. They are hungry all the time. Even if they just ate. Even if they've just told me they are not hungry. Even if they're already actively eating—they are hungry. So I try to keep healthy snacks on hand when we're out and about. While the definition of *healthy* has ebbed and flowed over the years (for instance, now it basically just means "not Doritos, but also sometimes Doritos"), you only need to make the rookie mistake of leaving the house without sustenance once before realizing you never want to experience a child's hangry meltdown ever again.

   No, nobody actually *wants* to eat these semi-warm, half-crumbled bag-o-snack snacks, but put any kid in a long-enough car rider line or preseason flag football information session, and suddenly that almost-obliterated school of cheddar fish starts to look pretty darn good.

3. Every Gift Card I've Ever Received

   Unless a cashier tells me the balance on my used gift card is absolute zero, I will hang on to that plastic parallelogram until someone pries it from my cold, dead fingers. You're telling me that on the off chance I stumble on two hours of free time and happen to be within a five-mile radius of a Nail Bar that I'm *not* going to want the $3.11 on this Secret Santa gift from 2017? Doubt it. I'd rather have my wallet bursting at its literal seams than throw away free money, so my purse has essentially become the Cave of Wonders for old, slightly used gift cards. *Only one may enter there; one whose worth lies far within. A mom, whose cuticles are looking rough.*

4. One Practically Empty ChapStick

   She's been through a lot, your purse ChapStick. If we look at the most current data, more than likely she's melted at least twice, and most studies have shown that she's 85 percent more likely than any other lip product to have been forgotten in the front pocket of one of your winter jackets. This is why I am fully committed to using every last millimeter of every tube of ChapStick that I buy. Does it sometimes end up hurting my dry lips when I push down really hard on the almost-empty tube so that a tiny smear of lubrication can glide on to my mouth? Sure. But while I have breath in my lungs, I am fully committed to standing by my classic cherry ChapStick—unless someone offers me some of their Burt's Bees, because that stuff is great.

5. Four Bobby Pins, an Expired Coupon, Two Matchbox Trucks, a Handful of Acorns and Rocks, and One Dried-Out Pen

Some might say that the bottom of a woman's purse is where unused items go to die, but truly advanced moms know it's actually where they go to be reincarnated and realize their true purpose:

What, honey? You cut your finger? Well, I don't have a Band-Aid because we used up everything in the first-aid kit when you tried to sled down that hill using a trash can lid, but I do have a semiclean coupon for buy-one-get-one Lender's Bagels. Listen, why don't you just roll your finger up in this and secure it with a bobby pin, and we'll address the situation properly once we get home.

You don't want to play at the playground anymore, sweetie? Well, your brothers are still playing, so why don't you put these acorns and rocks inside some Matchbox trucks and see which one stays in the longest when you race them down the slide.

I realize that this kind of purse dump is decidedly less sexy than what, say, Kristin Cavallari or Dame Judi Dench might pour out. But be honest, if you were stuck in a terrible traffic jam on your way back from an excruciatingly hot soccer tournament, who would you rather be stuck in a car with? Some fancy celeb with mint Tic Tacs and anti-aging skin creams, or a regular mom who almost definitely has a Pull-Up hidden somewhere, just in case?

CHAPTER 21

Cover Your Mouth

In the world of parenting small children with tiny immune systems, I've found that our family is often teetering in the space between "just getting over something" and "just about to catch something." It always seems like one child is still using their shirtsleeve as a Kleenex when the next one tells me their last poop was "like water." And if you're a parent or grew up with siblings, you know no one is ever sick with the same thing at the same time, creating a vast expanse of different germs and microbes comingling and replicating on countertops like they're on some kind of granite petri dish. I shudder to think what will happen when these different pathogens eventually mutate and splice with a Goldfish crumb and we get a

Pepperidge Farm variant of strep throat. I can almost hear Dr. Fauci's press conference now.

Of course, we all know the best way to ward off illness is with vigorous and thorough handwashing with warm, soapy water while we sing the "Happy Birthday" song. Twice. Sometimes, to add a little spice, I sing the ABCs. Armed with this potentially life-changing information, one would think families all across the world would be able to stop illness in its tracks.

Booger germs on your hands from the bus? Scrub-a-dub those bad boys with some Softsoap and say bye-bye to a two-week-long case of the sniffles!

Barfy bacteria under your fingernails? Drench those digits in some Dial and scour away a night spent clutching the toilet bowl.

It couldn't be simpler! Thank goodness we have this easy, foolproof way to arm ourselves against disease.

Except . . .

Have you ever watched a child wash their hands? Or, more specifically, have you ever watched a child be *told* to wash their hands and then observed what they think "washing hands" means? Because I have reason to believe that children's brains are hard-wired to think that when we say "wash your hands," what we actually mean is

Take your sweet time meandering to the bathroom. Turn on the water. Remember you need to pee. Pee. Don't flush. Get soap. Touch everything in the bathroom. Get more soap. Immediately rinse it off your hands without rubbing them

together or creating any germ-killing friction whatsoever. Dry your hands on your dirty clothes. Leave bathroom. Do not turn off water.

It's actually mind-blowing that COVID-19 was the first pandemic of our lifetime. Because kids (and honestly, some adults) are so gross that no matter how much we try to cough into our "chicken wing" or keep hand sanitizer at the ready, the laws of being a child dictate that snot from one kid's nose will find its way into another kid's mouth—and there isn't a damn thing we can do to stop it.[1]

Therefore, to brace myself for the inevitable call from the school nurse, I've compiled a list of the top four things my kids will come down with and subsequently pass on to your kids this school year.

1. The Twenty-Four-Hour Bug

    It begins with a watery poop. You know the kind—sounds like pee, smells way worse? It starts there and quickly morphs into a cycle of gastrointestinal explosions that turn your home into nothing more than a storehouse for Saltines and Gatorade.

    As a general rule, in our family everyone in the house will catch this stomach bug except me. Sure, I'll dry heave a little bit while rinsing crusty vomit out of the Tupperware bowl everyone's been barfing in, but

1. This might be a good time to pause and say there are actually some great ways to stop the spread of life-threatening diseases, and everyone deserves equal access to those measures. During a time when so many of us have felt scared and out of control, the absolute best thing we can do is take care of each other.

that doesn't really count. I will spend the duration of this illness running from child to child, making sure everyone is hydrated and has a turn to pick which episode of *Garfield* we watch next.

There's always a moment when I'm loading a third round of dirty sheets into the washing machine when I consider that maybe twenty-four hours off my feet wouldn't be so bad and contemplate taking a sip of contaminated Pedialyte, but then I remember I'm snack mom for T-ball on Saturday and I have a deadline for work and haven't finished prepping any of the teacher gifts for the end of the year, and I think better of it.

2. The "Headache"

In my eleven-odd years of parenting, I've found that this sneaky little sucker is usually brought on by a combination of dehydration and FOMO, generally rearing its ugly head after a late-night, sugar-fueled sleepover or when state-mandated testing days happen to coincide with the first warm day of spring. I want to be sympathetic and offer my kids Tylenol or a cold compress, but the really tricky part about having a "headache" is that it could mean that, yeah, my kid *might actually* be sick. But it could also mean they just pulled the exact same stunt I did at their age and are feigning a throbbing noggin to get out of learning about subtracting fractions. I'm no doctor, but the seasoned Dr. Google user in me generally suspects the latter.

3. The Endlessly Runny Nose

   From September to May, kids from the Florida Panhandle to the Pacific Northwest drip snot from their faces like tiny Saint Bernards hunting for hikers lost in the wilderness. And just like Saint Bernards, the majority of these kids will elect to use their tongues to deal with the snot, rather than reach for an available tissue or sleeve. Because kids, especially a-little-bit-sick kids, are animals. What is it about being slightly ill that renders children incapable of making rational choices?

   Where should I put this booger? Oh, I know, I'll wipe it on the side of the couch!

   Now what do I do with this other *booger? Oh, I know. I'LL EAT IT!*

   I'm terrified to think about what would happen with a third booger.

4. The Pediculus Humanus Capitis

   Also known as head lice. Did you just shudder? You did, didn't you? Because lice are every parent's nightmare. Not just because they are literal bugs living in your kids' hair, but because of all the insane amount of heavy lifting that comes with ridding your house of these teeny, tiny pests: The shampooing. The combing. The putting-every-stuffed-animal-in-a-garbage-bag-for-three-days-ing. It's a masterclass in household logistics, and if you fail, you have to repeat the class *and* you're itchy.

But take heart, my friends! While it's totally natural for the inevitable sick days to rock your world, turn your laundry pile into an insurmountable heap, and leave you looking like you haven't run a comb through your hair since back when *Grey's Anatomy* was actually good, there is still cause for (slight) celebration.

Because sick days are our chance to shine. We are the keeper and giver of all things "feel better." From non–socially distant snuggles on the couch to stocking up on the best flavors of sore throat–soothing popsicles,[2] we know the subtle touches that make being stuck at home sick just a liiiiiiittle bit of a treat. Even when an inopportune cough or fever throws a wrench in our grown-up plans, and especially when it breaks our heart to see our kids not feeling their best, there is something kind of sacred about taking care of our kids when they need us.

Even when you get puke on your shirt in the process.

---

2. Do not skimp on the *Paw Patrol* flavors.

CHAPTER 22

Roadside

When our older two boys were five and two, Brian and I decided to take a budget-friendly family road trip from Nashville to Boston. Now this may sound like a dream vacay to some, but I've reached a point in my life where I am comfortable sharing my deep disdain for multiday family car trips. If you're the kind of person who is into a wanderlust vacation vibe, I love that for you, but if we're talking about a drive of more than twelve hours *with* my children, you'd better believe I'm cashing in all my Southwest points to get my tush on an airplane. But back in my rookie mom days, I believed that being a "fun mom" meant doing things you hate. And so with a few Pinterest-inspired activities and a prayer, we loaded two weeks' worth of luggage into my tiny Nissan hatchback and hit the road.

If you've spent any time traveling by car across our great nation, you know there are a variety of obstacles you may encounter along your journey: putrid gas station bathrooms with no toilet paper, inflatable swimming pools flying off the roof of an oblivious Dodge Ram truck, "Repent" signs featuring Jesus Christ fighting off cartoon zombies,[1] and any number of other oddities that have become a part of the great American landscape. Being the type of mom who tends to plan for worst-case scenarios, I anticipated that our 1,100-mile journey would be littered with these types of encounters. I was on high alert. Our last family road trip had been waylaid after a tractor-trailer truck overturned and spilled raw chicken bits all over our route home. No matter how hard I've tried to repress that memory into the depths of my psyche (presumably beside all my other unsavory memories, like the time I accidentally laughed too hard at a joke about Beethoven and farted loudly at a piano recital), I don't think I'll ever fully get the smell of raw chicken mixed with car exhaust out of my nostrils.

White-knuckling it as Brian turned the car onto the on-ramp to I-65, I tried to defuse my anxiety by reminding myself that I'd planned for every possible scenario. We had snacks and wipes and books on tape, and if need be, I was prepared to perform a live-action version of *Charlotte's Web.*

---

1. This is a real sign I saw on I-95.

We were about two and a half hours into our northeast-bound trek when we decided it was time to stop for some outside-the-car nourishment at one of those trucker-friendly TA rest stops that boasted both hot showers and hot food. Essentially the Ritz Carlton of pit stops. This particular iteration of TA came equipped with a Subway, a Pizza Hut, *and* a Popeye's, which, in preschooler-speak, might as well have been a trifecta of Michelin-star restaurants. Oliver, who at five years old had experienced the processed cheesy goodness of Pizza Hut in the past, began prepping his younger brother for the wonder they'd behold as soon as their dad backed into a parking spot. (Yes, backed. Because that's how men park, and you all know it's true.)

With sweat pouring down our backs from thirty seconds in direct Tennessee summer sun, Brian and I unfastened the sixteen different buckles used to secure our children in their boosting, neck-securing, five-point car seats. We each took a child by the hand and made a mad dash between eighteen-wheelers to the front door and through the cosmic air-conditioner welcome blast that greets you at all roadside gas stations in the South. It's designed, I imagine, to cool you off and blast off any Chex Mix or Cheetos residue that may have attached itself to your person during your long drive.

The "food side," not to be confused with the "souvenir shop side," of this TA was incredibly busy for eleven thirty in the morning, so the kids and I were put on finding-a-non-sticky-table duty, while Brian secured a place for us in the pizza line. Oliver found us an 87-percent-clean four-top, and we sat down to wait for Brian to retrieve our boys' first official meal of vacation: a pair of sauce-covered dough circles with melted cheese that slid independently off the crust! Just like Italy intended. Presumably, once the kids had something to burn the roofs of their mouths with, Brian and I would then take shifts rotating through the Subway sandwich line to select which limp produce and waxy cheese to drape over our own crusty-ended dough ovals.

Finally, with four first official vacation meals in front of us, we commenced pigging out with grand fanfare by clinking our paper cups together and shouting "Cheers!" at least a dozen times. We covered our very full mouths while we giggled over Archie's silly two-year-old wiggle dance and wondered about which ride at our upcoming Dollywood pit stop was going to make me the dizziest.[2] It was good ol' fashioned family fun, and I was eating it up with a plastic truck-stop spork.

As I opened my pie hole to insert the final, semi-not-stale bite of my six-inch Subway sub, Oliver decided, as five-year-olds are wont to do, that it would be a good time to pivot to an entirely new line of conversation.

"Mom! Mom!"

I glanced up to see my son gesturing wildly toward the line for Pizza Hut. "Mom! Mom! Look! Over there. At that guy standing there. *That guy!* The one at the end of the line. With the backpack. Him."

---

2. It was all of them. All the rides.

He has always been very specific, my son Oliver. When he was four, he told me that it's the taste not the texture that caused his aversion to specific types of cheese. He is also always generous enough to remind me when I've contradicted myself regarding a specific household rule or bedtime-related proclamation. So when he points out a stranger, I always know *exactly* which stranger he means.

While Oliver was gesticulating wildly in the direction of some poor soul, both Brian and I started to feel very conspicuous, as parents do. The elderly couple who had been smiling sentimentally in our direction while we cheersed our lunch, turned back to their meals reminded of why they were glad to no longer be navigating difficult parenting scenarios.

I side-glanced to my left, trying to catch a glimpse of what had my son making such a fuss. What would I find? A heavily tattooed traveler? A man with a service dog? Not that there is anything especially unusual about these potential scenarios, but each would require that I respond with a socially and age-appropriate answer, within seconds. While I collected my thoughts, nervous sweat began to pool on my upper lip.

You got this Kelly. You're definitely not going to give the perfect response, but you've got something close to the right answer in there somewhere.[3]

Armed with what I thought was a pretty decent arsenal of possible responses, I swiveled my neck until I saw a man with long, scraggly hair and a worn-out, overstuffed, dirty

3. This is *now* Kelly talking to *then* Kelly. I'm really into time travel right now, *okay*?!

camo backpack, waiting in the line for some lunch. Brian and I locked eyes; it was go time.

Alright, so homelessness, a person without housing, life choices, everyone's experiences are different, maybe this man was just going through a rough patch? You know, thanks to the demands of modern capitalism, many people are overextending their credit, and that can have a ripple effect that is hard to come back from—especially if someone is also underwater due to outrageous medical bills, also Jesus said to love everyone. . . . Okay, I sort of got this.

What I feared the most in this scenario was speaking some kind of accidental internal bias over my son. What if I said the wrong thing and Oliver carried what his mom told him for the rest of his life? As a kid, I'd had my own struggles with people speaking things over me about my body, and that haunted me until, well, it still haunts me, which had to be a part of why I was so shaken up about handling this situation correctly. The things we say become the things our kids say—and then repeat to their friends.

Thoughts swirling in my head, I turned back to my son, who was now literally pointing at this man clear across the gas station, just in time to hear him say, "Do you see that guy, Mom? Isn't he *awesome?* Look at his *backpack*!"

Immediately, the panic over my son's potential judgment of another human being vanished, only to shed light on another, less altruistic, reason for my internal freak-out: What would these other truck-stop patrons gnawing on their tiny Pizza Hut pizzas think of *me*? Was I a good mom? Was I raising open-minded kids? Was I savvy enough to parent my way through this very public situation without hurting anyone? Everything was about me and the feigned perfection I was trying to maintain with this group of strangers . . . and arguably everyone else I'd ever met in my entire life.

> Stupid social pressures and gender-
>   normative mom guilt
> make me do all kinds of dumb stuff I don't
>   even wanna do,
> like pretend to have it all together
> when I really just want to be
> the kind of mom
> who forces her kids to share their pizza
>   crusts with her,
> even if they don't want to.
>
> —A POEM, FOR MOMS

As the initial tension of the moment eased, Brian and I traded relieved glances and agreed that, yes, that guy was awesome, and his backpack was very cool. Oliver was supremely satisfied and returned to eating pizza and not sharing his crusts with me. Using our best quiet adult voices, Brian and I used parent code to share our disbelief about how easily we had gotten off and how beautifully free of judgment children are before our gross opinions get projected all over them. And I balled up my moment of self-discovery and shoved it way down deep in my suitcase to deal with on another day.

Because, after all, we were on vacation.

CHAPTER 23

Radio Silence

For most of my life, God didn't talk to me.

As I'd grown up Catholic, the two of us conducted most of our business on Sundays via the long-winded rebukes of various parish priests, while I counted to see how many bald guys were at Mass that weekend. Comb-overs didn't count, and bonus points if they had something weird growing on their scalp. I don't think God really liked that part, but he does all things for the good of those who love him, so I can only assume he put those balding men in my eyeline for a reason.

My memory on the issue is a little hazy, but judging by the number of withering looks I endured from my parents during Mass each week, I'd venture to say that I didn't do a spectacular job of covering up the fact that I was not actually paying attention while our family was at church. Could you blame me? Dad said we were getting bagels afterwards. Who could think about anything else? Regardless of my preoccupation with future bagels or sending my mom telepathic signals to let us leave after communion, I knew God was there, probably just waiting for me to grow up a little bit so we could chat about important stuff, like ending world hunger and why *Dr. Quinn, Medicine Woman* didn't get renewed for a seventh season. Until then, I would focus my attention on spotting more bald heads and hoping for funny names during the Prayer of the Faithful.

As I've grown in my faith, I've unpacked that a big piece of the reason I never felt personally connected to God growing up was because of the gatekeeperish nature of my Religion. That's religion with a big R, not just the Catholic faith inherently. It's a practice spread across denominations, this sentiment that we parishioners needed another human being to act as an intermediary between us and Jesus in order to instruct and inform our relationship with him.[1] It was an approach that always made me feel like God was keeping me at arm's length. That I wasn't good or worthy enough to have access to the *real* goods, just whatever the church deemed appropriate to share during the week's carefully selected mis-

1. Priests, pastors, etc. are great at helping us explore our faiths, but relationships with God are personal, so I'd contend their teaching should be only a part of how we define our faiths. And if we *are* going to look for church leaders to help inform how we experience the world, then maybe us gals would like to hear from someone who isn't a fifty-year-old white man every Sunday.

sal readings. This was especially difficult during the years my OCD was at its peak, when a reading from the letter of Paul to the Corinthians could trigger an intense shame response about being rude or selfish, and made any attempt at reading the Bible feel like trying to understand Shakespeare, which, as we all know, is essentially impossible unless you have a tenth-grade English teacher leaning over your shoulder, decoding every single line.

Like many people, after leaving the church where I grew up, I spent much of my twenties searching for the "right" church that would create a space where I felt safe to explore my relationship with God. A place that would give me permission to ask questions or express doubts. Did you guys know that those places are crazy hard to find? Admittedly, part of the problem was me. As someone who has only recently discovered that it's okay to approach my relationship with God in whatever way feels most authentic and comfortable to me, I had mistakenly gone church hopping, looking for a community that would do all the heavy lifting for me. But what I discovered was that no amount of "perfect" church, building or body, can manifest a good relationship with God.

That's on me.

Early in our marriage, Brian and I found a church where both of us felt at home, which was no small feat considering our differing faith backgrounds—his in the Evangelical Bible Belt and mine in the Catholic Corridor.[2] God was beginning to become a more palpable presence in my life, but even with that welcomed shift you could've knocked me down with a palm frond when, during the second chorus of "In Christ Alone," on one seemingly random Sunday in 2016, I had the almost audible thought of, *We should adopt*.

My first response, Christian woman that I am, was, *Abso*bleeping*lutely, we should not*. I was immediately overwhelmed by the idea of it; and that was all that it was—an idea. Wasn't it? Just an idea in my head? It wasn't like God was *actually* speaking into my life, because that would be nuts. I rationalized my fears by assuring myself that although Brian and I *had* talked about the possibility of adopting, that was way back when we were first dating, and when I had said that "maybe I'd want to adopt someday," I meant, like, in twenty years, when I was a *real* grown-up.

After decades of waiting and wishing to hear from God, I couldn't shake the feeling that he was finally speaking to me. But like every cast member of *The Truman Show*, I didn't breathe a word about what was actually going on to anyone. Instead, I cynically asked God to up his game. I demanded that he tell me again, and louder this time. And then I sat back and waited for radio silence.

2. I just made this term up, but I think it's really good.

Three days later, our family of four went out to dinner. As our five- and two-year-olds raced Hot Wheels cars all over the table, all of us wincing every time they *almost* spilled their beloved restaurant lemonades, Brian and I started up a conversation about how life was good. Finances were good. Marriage was good. Kids were good.

And then he put his elbows on the table, leaned over, and said, "So what should we do now? Like, adopt a kid or something?"

And my chin dropped to the floor, which was sticky, because our kids had finally spilled their lemonades.

I had not uttered a single word to him about my first-ever conversation with God earlier that week. And here he was, bringing up adoption—something we hadn't discussed in years. Confirming what I'd asked God to do—to speak louder. To tell me he was real. And so right there, over sticky laminated menus, we started talking about adding a third child to our family, with stars in our eyes and absolutely zero insight into the weight and nuance this conversation carried.

Several weeks of discussions during late-night Googling sessions and lunch dates with other adoptive families later, we started filling out the paperwork to formally begin the adoption process. Twelve pounds of it, to be exact. Most of it photocopied after work in the teacher's prep room, which is definitely against school policy, but do you know how much OfficeMax charges for twelve pounds of paper? Dunder Mifflin would never.

Rookie Mistakes

When you're in the process of adopting, either domestically or internationally, you rightly go through a rigorous screening protocol. This includes home visits from the adoption agency caseworker assigned to your family. These visits are essentially to make sure you have working smoke detectors, carbon monoxide detectors, or any other life or death detector deemed necessary. Our agency told us over and over not to stress about these visits—that they wanted to see us in our natural element and have a chance to meet our two biological children. Nothing more. So obviously, as one does, I cleaned my house like the pope was coming and spent two days trying to decide which pair of church khakis my kids should wear for the occasion. It wasn't enough that our caseworker be able to check off all the boxes on her forms; she needed to write "I like these people! They are cool and fun!" in the margins.

When the day of our official home visit arrived, our caseworker entered a home that I can honestly say I'd never been in before. The entire house had been scrubbed so thoroughly that I am positive every single visible surface was one that hadn't existed the day before. So it was with total confidence that I flung the front door open and welcomed her to our absolutely never-dirty, always-perfect home. Our caseworker carried a clipboard full of forms and wore a flowing dress that swung across our sparkling floors as she made her way to our kitchen table. She was friendly and disarming, asking questions about Oliver and Archie and our normal daily routines.

"They're great. They're both really great. And our normal routine is also great. Breakfast. Bus. School. Play. Dinner. Bath. Bed. We love a nice, normal routine. WE ARE NORMAL AND GREAT!"

And then she asked if we kept all medicines and sharp objects up high or under lock and key. I assured her that "yes, of course" we'd never take risks with our children's safety. We were extremely good and thoughtful parents. And then our five-year-old shouted from across the room.

"What about the steak knives? I can get those! Like soooooo easily! And they are sharrrrrrp sharp!"

A few rehomed kitchen knives and carefully placed child locks later, our home study was approved, and we were on our way to welcoming a little boy or girl from the east-central African country of Burundi into our family.

While we waited for the Central Authority Matching Committee in Bujumbura to meet and pair us with our future son or daughter, we educated ourselves about Burundian culture and what we could expect from walking through a transracial adoption and becoming a transracial family. Two things we as white parents could not possibly understand the weight of until we experienced them with our child (or ever), but we read the required readings and did the required trainings because we had to check the required boxes.

And then we waited.

We waited for a year, dreaming of the child who would join our family. We talked with Oliver and Archie about what they might look like, sound like, *be* like—all the while, without us knowing, a very different story was being written for us on an entirely different continent altogether.

On a drizzly morning in May 2017, just as school was letting out for the summer, my cell phone rang. It was our caseworker. There was no news about our Burundi matching process. What else was new? But her tone seemed too cheery to be calling with no news. With excitement and just a touch of hesitation in her voice, she began to tell me about an eighteen-month-old little boy in the Philippines whose birth mom had tragically and unexpectedly passed away just days after he was born. With no other family available to care for him, after being released from the hospital, this little boy had been sent to a state-run orphanage and had been waiting there ever since. She asked if we would be willing to read his file, and I said we would.

Brian and I sat together and read over the little boy's comprehensive and lengthy medical file over lunch at one of those casual dining places that serves 3,000-calorie salads. There was a lot to digest (physically and emotionally), but as we scrolled through the information in front of us, we both felt strangely calm. A calmness that I have to believe was rooted in the fact that the file we were reading detailed some disabilities that fit exactly into the wheelhouse of my experience as a speech-language pathologist.

Was this God speaking to me again? I couldn't be sure.

I thought I had heard his message clearly the first time, but this seemed like a pretty significant change of plans, even for him. Could our family really change course and start all over again? And what about all the paperwork? Oh, my God, the paperwork! I could feel my anxiety rising at the prospect of having to rearrange all the color-coded binders and folders that I'd spent the last year meticulously organizing. Undoing everything that I'd believed was right to start way back at the beginning felt overwhelming, but it was becoming clear that a course correction was necessary.

"We're going to do this, aren't we?" Brian asked after lunch, as he put his truck in gear. As much as I wanted to say yes, feelings of self-doubt and fear were starting to creep in: *Was I a good enough mom for this? A good enough therapist?* This little boy had already been through so much in his short life. I couldn't bear the thought of him drawing the short straw in the adoptive parents department.

For reasons I can't quite explain, instead of making my go-to rookie mistake of giving in to my fears, this time I did something different. I turned to Brian and said, "Yeah, let's do it."

Because a decade ago, I had that unexplainable feeling that I should change careers and go back to school for a very specific degree, to be able to help children with very specific needs. A surprising instinct that I couldn't wholly rationalize at the time, but decided to follow, because I couldn't get it out of my mind. That happens sometimes, doesn't it? Those persistent little thoughts that you just can't shake end up shaping the very trajectory of your entire life. And as it happens, years later one of those very feelings would lead me right to our third little boy, living halfway around the world.

Which makes me realize now that God has been talking to me all along.

CHAPTER 24

The Plane!

I am not a good flyer. I used to be, back when I was a child and spent most flights looking for Care Bears living in the clouds. Back then, I loved air travel. The glitz and glamour of ordering a Coke off a cart and getting your own two-foot-by-two-foot cubicle of personal space! Ooh là là! I even loved turbulence and trying to predict the exact moment the pilot would turn on the "fasten seatbelt sign." I was pretty good at that too. I usually timed my guess within just a couple of bumps.

Now that I'm an adult, hurtling through the sky in a metal tube feels . . . less good. While I genuinely try my hardest not to get into this headspace, on any given flight I mentally prepare for catastrophe no less than five or six times, more if we're flying over an ocean. I don't know what it is, but there's just something about the idea of disappearing over the Pacific that I'd really like to distance myself from. But seven miles above the ground, you have no control—not even over who you share your row of seats with in your coffin, I mean plane.

It is no wonder, then, that as Brian and I stood in the jetway line at LAX to board our fourteen-hour flight (mostly over oceans) to Manila, I was praying harder than a child trying to convince his parents to let him have a sleepover. I wasn't necessarily praying not to crash, although that would be a nice bonus. I was mostly praying to not be terrified. Because I was oh-so terrified. Not of the *actual* life-changing event waiting for us in the Philippines, but of a hypothetical scenario that would lead to my obituary reading something like:

Kelly Bandas, survived by her entire family, died tragically when she was the only passenger on Flight 341 to be sucked from the airplane when a high-flying pelican crashed into her window.

The other passengers waiting in line, including four American guys I assumed were heading overseas for a couple of weeks of "killer zip-lining and day drinking, *Bruh*," seemed frighteningly unaware of how precarious our circumstances were. Had none of them ever watched *Lost*? Did they not know we could potentially be walking toward our final hours? Would there be a doctor onboard as capable, yet as disarmingly handsome, as Matthew Fox? I needed answers! And a Valium. I probably needed a Valium.[1]

---

1. It's been my experience that most adoptive parents aren't allowed to have the slightest whisper of mental-health difficulties. My doctor and I had signed

It's true I was probably slightly more on edge because, after two-and-a-half years of red tape, Brian and I were finally allowed to travel to bring our son CJ home. As usual, if Brian had any travel anxiety, he didn't show it. Years of playing gigs on the road had made him impervious to any fears of flying. He'd likely have his nose in four or five different books for the entire flight, while I held my breath all the way to customs. My only hope would be distracting-enough in-flight movies, but my hopes weren't high. And so I prayed. Really hard and really fast:

Please don't let me be scared. Please send me a sign to calm me down.

Please don't let me be scared. Please send me a sign to calm me down.

Please don't let me be scared. Please send me a sign to calm me down.

I prayed all the way to my seat, adding a final, "Love, Kelly Bandas. Amen" when my neck pillow and I plopped down on the ruddy-colored Philippines Air upholstery somewhere toward the back half of the plane. I scrunched up my knees, creating six millimeters of extra space so Brian and his backpack could slide past me into the window seat, and was left with a giant question mark as to who I'd be spending the next fourteen hours sitting beside.

"Mabuhay," the flight attendants welcomed us over the PA system, before asking everyone to take their seats to ensure

---

documentation that I was "totally cured" of my OCD, and therefore I couldn't ask her to prescribe me any antianxiety medication.

an on-time departure. *Mabuhay. Mabuhay.* I pulled out my phone, which was still hanging on by a thread to the terminal Wi-Fi, and typed "Mabuhay" into Google Translate:

"Long live."[2]

That had to be a good sign, right?

As the engines roared to life, the four dudes I'd seen at the top of the jetway entered our section of the cabin. Surely with hundreds of seats on the plane, there was only a small chance that I'd end up sitting next to one of them. The thought of suffering through fourteen hours of listening to some entitled twentysomething in Rainbow sandals talk about his "epic vacay" was enough to kick my anxiety back into red-alert mode. So I started praying again:

Please don't let me be scared. Please send me a sign to calm me down.

Please don't let me be scared. Please send me a sign to calm me down.

And in God's own subtly hilarious way, that is exactly what he did.

"Hi, I'm Michael," the Ed Hardy T-shirt-wearing "brojan" said. Now, this kid's name could've been anything, especially Chad, but it wasn't. It was Michael. The name of the archangel who acts as chief protector and evil-caster-outer, who kicked Satan's butt and basically chills in heaven waiting to do God's next BA errand. And I could've written this all off as coincidence, but after we exchanged a few airline-passenger

2. In English, "Mabuhay" literally translates to "long live," but it is a formal greeting generally used to mean "welcome."

pleasantries, Michael asked, "Is it cool with you guys if I pray for us before the flight?"

Normally, the thought of praying with a stranger in public would be number one on my Things to Avoid list, but there was something about *this* stranger, showing up immediately after my private panic prayer, that made this interaction significantly less youth-pastory than I would have anticipated. And so he prayed for us. Many times, in fact, over the course of our flight. He prayed for safety when we hit wild turbulence over the Pacific and for our first meeting with CJ after we told him the reason for our trip. And if that wasn't proof enough, he ate not one crumb of food during the entire daylong flight. Not a pretzel. Not a peanut. Not a hundred-calorie pack of Oreo slims. Nothing. In my experience, there are only two kinds of beings who don't boredom-eat during travel: angels/ghosts and people who do sudokus in pen. Michael never picked up a writing utensil or said "BOO!" so I can only assume he was an angel. Or at least someone sent by God, as an angel by proxy.

After our wheels touched down in Manila (no clapping on international flights), we never saw Michael again, but Brian and I talked about him that night in our hotel room as we lay down to sleep for a few hours before we'd meet our son the very next morning. We still had one final flight from Manila to his home in Leyte, about an hour south of Manila. The short flight promised to be on one of those small island-hopper planes that usually gave me even worse anxiety than flying on a massive jumbo jet, but as I laid my head down on the overstuffed hotel pillow and started to stream an episode of *30 Rock* to lull me to sleep, I wasn't worried at all about our flight.

I go back and forth about whether Michael was a miracle. In the grand scheme of Things That Deserve a Miracle, my being a nervous flyer doesn't really feel like it ought to be at the top of the list. That slot should belong to things that *really* matter, not some woman's little, insignificant anxieties. Although I suppose if God passed out miracles based on who *deserved* them, there probably wouldn't be many miracles at all. Maybe that's what makes them miracles, the very idea that God shows up for us in all kinds of ways, when we didn't do anything to earn it.

So yeah, I think I do believe Michael was a miracle. Because in my experience, God tends to show up when things are turbulent, and most importantly, he knows me intimately enough to understand I'd get a good laugh out of an angel in an Ed Hardy T-shirt.

CHAPTER 25

TMI

If you're nosy enough, you can find out pretty much anything these days. No, not nosy. That's a bit harsh, I think. Curious. Yes, that sounds better. I think most of us are motivated by curiosity when we type things into our Internet search bar, like "Why isn't Prince Harry bald?" and "Ben Affleck and J.Lo back together + images + 2021."

Feeling intrigued by other people's personal stories isn't a new phenomenon, although Google images certainly makes it easier these days. We human beings have been fascinated by each other's behavior since *Australopithecus* was all like, "Whatchu guys doin'?" when *Homo habilis* started using simple tools.

Equally un-new is our desire to share our own stories and make our experiences known and heard by the people around us. One might argue that's the entire reason social media and books like this one even exist—because there's really no more powerful tool than sharing our stories with each other to help us feel connected with one another.

"You're telling me you experienced a life-changing event that resulted in a change in your baseline emotional state? STFU. Me too!"

Boom. Connection.

But where this desire for connection starts to get tricky is when our stories become interwoven with the stories of other people—our kids, parents, in-laws, and so forth—and our desire to share can mean we're sharing a piece of someone else's story that isn't ours to give.

During the years leading up to CJ becoming a part of our family, I wrote *a lot* about my experience as a potential adoptive parent. I wrote about the heartache of waiting and the disappointment of various roadblocks throughout our process. And in a way, I semi-excuse this because those essays were a helpful tool in processing a difficult time. But in another less excusable way, many parts of those essays weren't mine to share.

When Brian and I met CJ in person for the very first time, he was three years old and wearing an orange T-shirt that said Yokohama Truckers with shorts to match. He was running happily around the room he shared with seven other children, playing chase with his friend and laughing loudly, the same way he does now with his big brothers when he gets *really* tickled by something. As CJ and his friend ricocheted off cribs and crawled under beds, Brian stood in the doorway and watched, while me and my amped-up emotions started having a cute little stress-induced migraine. This was *the* moment; the one we'd been waiting for and praying about for years—and what? Now we were all expected to formally meet as parents and child while the staff at RSCC 8[1] watched and graded each of our reactions?

> **ME:** *Hello, CJ. It's a pleasure to make your acquaintance. We'll be your parents now.*
>
> **CJ:** *That sounds great! And I also have no follow-up questions.*
>
> **ME:** *Here's some candy!*

While I was still feeling somewhat paralyzed by the reality that in a few moments Brian and I would officially have another child, some of the staff started shouting at CJ to get his attention and pointing in our direction: "Mommy! Daddy! Mommy! Daddy!" They wanted to give us that picture-perfect first meeting that every adoptive story necessitates. The one the family eventually posts on Facebook to mark the *ending*

---

1. The Reception and Study Center for Children was a state-run home for children without families able to care for them. CJ's caregivers there loved him deeply and cared for him so well. We are forever grateful.

of their "adoption journey." And although their attempts to connect us were well-intentioned, they truly had almost no effect because

a. we were total strangers. Not Mommy and Daddy; and
b. CJ's only hearing aid had been lost during a monsoon months before, and he could barely hear a word they were saying.

But still, he smiled at us, hesitantly. And eventually he let Brian put him on his shoulders, after deciding that this big, tall man was going to be a lot of fun. I watched and smiled from the wings, not wanting to overwhelm the situation, but once some of the other children descended on Brian for piggyback rides of their own, CJ indulged me in a game of hide-and-seek. As I scrambled across the tiled floors on my hands and knees, scurrying to find a hiding spot easily accessible to three-year-old eyes, I could hear CJ quietly repeating the only word I'd heard from him all day, "Wow." And I couldn't blame him, because that's how I felt too.

If that were the end of the story, it would seem nice. Like, you know, #adoptionrocks.

And it does.

Sort of.

Until he is old enough to begin to fully process that day, I can't understand what the experience of meeting me was like for CJ. Yes, Brian and I were nice and we had lollipops, but that didn't make us his mom and dad. His mom was Jay Ann, and CJ had already lost her.

A few short hours after meeting CJ, Brian and I left the children's home to bring him back to the hotel where we were staying. CJ came along willingly, carrying a small backpack full of his belongings. He'd folded his things meticulously all by himself and tucked them inside, proud to bring them along. He bravely sat on Brian's lap in the back of the van as we bumped along the crowded roads, eyes wide, but not making a sound. Because CJ had no way of hearing or communicating with us, no one was able to explain to him where we were going or what was about to happen, but as soon as we made it to our hotel and the door of our room clicked closed and he burst into tears, I knew that he knew. CJ cried in my arms that afternoon until he fell asleep from exhaustion, his tiny whimpers easing only as he drifted off into a deep sleep.

Even though this was the day that we became a family, this was also a very scary day for CJ. Because as I've come to understand since knowing my youngest son, while adoption is love, adoption is also trauma. And if that sounds like I'm straddling a very polarized fence, that's because I am. As the great Bruce Springsteen would say,[2] in order to be real adults, we need to be able to hold two seemingly contradictory truths in our minds at the same time and understand that both can be true.

2. This concept can be traced back well before Bruce's time, but I heard him say this during an interview recently, and it sounds best in his gravelly voice.

Our family had jumped into adoption headfirst, eager to help find a family for a little boy or girl with no one available to care for them. And although some people might disagree, I don't believe this was wrong. But what I didn't see then that I can clearly see now is that, in an effort to find permanency and support for children without families, culturally we've romanticized adoption, exalting adoptive parents as altruistic saviors who've "saved" their children. And wow, as a potential adoptive parent, that romantic sentiment felt really, really good. Good enough that I didn't think to question myself as I clack-a-lacked on my keyboard, blogging away about a son who I'd never even met and telling *his* story, not mine. I just sat at my desk, eating animal crackers[3] and basking in all the comments and well-wishes from curious strangers who'd read our story online and were cheering us on toward the finish line. A finish line that would mean a culmination of years of waiting for me and yet another trauma for CJ.

I can be a great mom to CJ. And Brian can be a great dad. And our family can do everything in our power to give him a loving home with every opportunity that he wouldn't have had without a nuclear family, but—and because he's my son and I love him deeply, this guts me to type—I know that the best thing for CJ would've been to have a life with his biological

3. A quick animal cracker tutorial that nobody asked for. The *only* way to eat animal crackers is to bite off their legs and head, one by one, and then suck on their body until it dissolves in your mouth. I will not be taking questions.

parents. Nothing can replace that. So now it's my responsibility, as one of his moms, to learn from people who've lived an experience like his. I don't have all the answers or know all the things, but what I do know is that it's my job to help my son let his story unfold the way he wants—to embrace his birth culture and his Deaf culture and affirm that those parts of him are rich and beautiful and important. And to never make him feel like he was "lucky" to be adopted.

When CJ first came home, in an effort to be transparent and authentic, I was very open on social media about the challenges our family was facing. To be very honest, I regret it. Not because it was fake or "for the 'gram," but because the brush I was using painted me as the savior in his story, and I'm no more CJ's savior than I am Archie's or Oliver's. I'm just the woman who gets to be their mom.

These days, I like to share regular mom stuff: lost teeth, silly dancing, and running through sprinklers. I like to talk about how CJ wakes up singing in the morning and giggles his way to bed at night. About how he is fearless and loves football and has learned two languages in under two years. And how he is one of my three sons, who I would cross the world for a million times over. When more difficult moments arise, we walk through those with close friends and family, those who know our boys and have a real relationship with them. I'm still honest and real when it comes to parenting truths (like thinking Monday is the best day of the week, and I will die on that hill), but those stories are mine to tell.

And CJ's are his.

Part 4

The Realizing-That-Getting-Your-Act-Together-Takes-Your-Whole-Life Part

"Hey, Alexa, Order More Toilet Paper"

CHAPTER 26

The Uncles J and J

One of my grandfathers spent his entire adult life working as a commercial artist. The other worked as a cattle rancher for more than thirty years. Both men were the sons of immigrants, taught to show up to the same job, day after day, year after year, in order to provide a good life for their family.

I am now thirty-six years old and, to date, have had no less than ten different jobs. That's excluding, of course, the odds-and-ends type of gigs one tends to leave off a professional resume, like "writer for a local magazine that went out of print after one issue" or "part-time assistant at a vintage T-shirt startup." I don't know if this is the norm, but I suspect that there's a good chance many of us older millennials spent much of our twenties and thirties searching for "the perfect job"—a cultural shift I lovingly refer to as the Uncle J Phenomenon.

You'll recall (I hope) that during *Full House*'s eight-year run, Uncles Joey and Jesse were forever changing career paths, convincing a generation of young people that they, too, could seamlessly transition from pest exterminator to pop star to drivetime radio DJ with nary a hiccup or COBRA coverage along the way. It wasn't *intentional* messaging, necessarily. I think the folks at ABC were more interested in monetizing the Olsen twins than they were in inspiring the next generation of working-class Americans. But inspire us they did! The owners of the Smash Club and Double J Creative Services (that's two more jobs!) stirred within our impressionable frontal lobes the idea that even after you hit the arbitrary age that makes you a grown-up, it's okay to change the trajectory of your life.

This shift in cultural ideology is largely the reason I felt comfortable shifting from careers in baseball to country music to speech pathology to the work I do now—a hybrid career I've lovingly dubbed *Stay-at-Home Comedienne*. These days some might call this a sense of millennial entitlement, but I choose to see it through a different lens. At one time I, too, was under the impression that by twenty-five most of us should have both feet firmly planted in a *forever* job. That career hopping was a young person's game, and the only reason anyone in their thirties would leave a good-paying job was because they were a quitter who didn't have their act together. And there was no excuse for that, because by your thirties you're done growing up. You are a fully loaded adult. No more updates required.

Now this kind of thinking might make sense if any of us could claim to be anything but a rookie human being. Maybe if we were given a go or two at life before having to make firm decisions about how we'd spend most of our days here on earth, we could make slightly more informed decisions, but because this is everyone's first attempt at personhood, it stands to reason that maybe Uncles Jesse and Joey had the right idea. If you're following a path that dead-ends, make like Ranger Joe and take another trail.

After years of chasing the unachievable perfect work–life balance, I was starting to feel burned out at my job as a preschool speech-language pathologist. I still loved the work itself, but between the demands of therapy and family and students and my own children, I was beginning to feel like an old, dried-out kitchen sponge. The one that you look at and think, *I don't want to waste that sponge, but there's bits of dried scrambled egg stuck to it. I know—I'll get out a new sponge but leave this one on the edge of the sink for another day or two and then throw it in the garbage.*

That was me. Two days away from becoming total human trash and knowing that I needed to do something different. It was a worrisome feeling, because if I left my job that meant I couldn't use it as my "I help people/I'm a good person" crutch anymore. And I loved that crutch. It made me feel important and smart, and, like, even if I really messed up in other areas of my life, I had a trump card that would remind everyone that I had value. It was my "Get Out of Hell Free" card, and I was desperate to hang on to it.

For so many of us, it's become increasingly difficult to separate our identity from whatever it says on our business cards,[1] and as much as I wanted to ignore my dried-out sponge feeling and continue to base my worth on a job that wasn't serving me anymore, I knew my current shriveled state was trying to tell me something—that I was becoming a new version of myself, and I needed to figure out whatever it was that I needed to resaturate. As it turned out, what I needed was a full-sized bottle of lotion, some raw chicken, and a wooden spoon.

While mindlessly scrolling Instagram a while back, I came across a #sponsored celebrity post for one of those FabFitFun boxes. You know, the ones with the *full-size* beauty products that even us normal uggos can purchase for the shockingly low, low price of $49.99? Yeah, those. There was always something about those ads that felt even more disingenuous than most—something about the messaging or the cost that always came off as aggressively tone deaf. Truly, I have more faith in the youths on YouTube who try to sell my kids moon sand

1. Ha ha ha. Remember business cards?

than I do in the guys and gals who try to convince me I need a subscription box to moisturize my feet properly. There's absolutely nothing wrong with influencers[2] sharing products they love with their followers, but I always felt like the idea of a celebrity paying fifty dollars for a subscription box of stuff that will most likely end up in their assistant's junk drawer to be supremely hilarious.

Even though this kind of ad had bugged me for months, there was something about this particular high-gloss iteration, on this particular day, that really wound me up. Maybe it was just excess ring light ricocheting off a bottle of collagen lip-plumping serum, but I swear a lightbulb went off in my head. As a fun little treat for myself, I was going to make a parody video about FabFitFun for my own Instagram page.

I walked around my house grabbing all the necessary props: a wooden spoon, a giant bottle of store-brand lotion, and a huge Tupperware container of some of Brian's marinating chicken from the fridge. Then, with all my accoutrements in place, I leaned my phone up against a stack of books and hit "record." I made funny jokes and terrible ones. I did perfect takes and some truly awful ones. Occasionally, one of my kids would walk in, see me cry-laughing, all alone, save my inverted reflection in the phone, and slowly back out of the room. Mom had gone and lost her mind. And maybe I had a

2. In a world that is constantly trying to cut down the female-dominated world of influencers, I am definitely not here to do that. I think influencers are bad-ass, hustling entrepreneurs who inform a large portion of my purchasing decisions. Give them all the clicks!

little bit, but I was having a great time doing it. Just me and my amateur comedy sketch.

When I posted the video the next day, it didn't go viral or get thousands of likes. Not even close. But to my surprise, it did something even better. It showed me that doing something that brought this evolving version of myself joy was actually really important. That finding space and time to be silly and laugh was life giving. And that giving my kids that kind of mom was going to be a priority for me moving forward. I wasn't setting my sights on becoming the next Laura Clery or Tiffany Jenkins; I just wanted to give myself some room to breathe and get to know the person I was becoming—someone who didn't derive their self-worth from her title on her email signature.

In the two years since making this career shift, I've filmed over 200 comedy sketches. Some were funny. Some definitely weren't. But every single one made me a little bit braver about who I was becoming and a little bit more certain of the kind of person I want to be. Maybe I'd write comedy sketches until my wrinkled, arthritic fingers can no longer press the keys of my keyboard, or maybe like my beloved Uncle Js, I would reboot myself twenty years from now. The important thing was, I realized, that although there was nothing wrong with the road I was traveling before, it was time to take the next exit and reevaluate my route. Any maybe try taking the scenic route for once.

CHAPTER 27

Moms Demand

When I was in elementary school, my favorite thing to do at recess was to hold foot races with other kids. In full blue jeans and half-tied sneakers, we would tear back and forth across the open field behind the playground for our entire allotted twenty minutes of freedom. My hair was cut too short for a proper ponytail, so my "high" speeds caused every carefully placed barrette and clip to lose its grip and sent my hair flying wildly around my head, creating knots within snarls within tangles. But who cared? Because did you see that? I was *flying*!

Once the end-of-recess whistle blew, signaling the return to *boring* social studies or *stupid* math, we'd all return to our classrooms red-faced and undeodorized to tell our nonracing

friends the dramatic tales of our victories or, even more excitingly, our robberies—the finish lines in these races being notoriously fickle.

Win or lose, you could catch a high during these races—a surge of endorphins that could make you feel powerful enough to tackle even the excruciatingly boring lesson on acute angles or, worse yet, the water cycle. I still chase that high. Not in playground foot races anymore, although if anyone wants to meet up in an open field one day and shake the lead out, I'd be game. No, now I've taken to longer, lonelier runs along the pavement of suburbia, past the Jiffy Lube and the Chick-fil-A with the really long drive-thru.

With no other runners nipping at my heels, I have to trick my brain into getting psyched up by listening to pop music from the early nineties or a really good true-crime podcast. And sometimes, if the playlist or Sarah Koenig hit *just* right, I can catch that same high from all those years ago—that high that makes me feel like every thought I think is *gold*, and all my ideas are the most brilliant ideas anyone has ever had.

It was during one of these runner's highs a few years back that I decided that, yes, I would take a friend up on her invitation to join her at a Moms Demand Action (MDA) meeting. MDA is an incredible gun-sense organization that is anti–gun violence and pro–gun safety. They do incredible work, and I was going to be a part of it. I would sign up for all the committees and legislative actions and marches, and *I was going to change the world!*

In the wake of Sandy Hook and Stoneman Douglas,

suburbia no longer felt out of the reach of mass acts of violence. My privileged thought process of "that'll never happen here" collapsed as I watched mothers and fathers weep for their children on the news; kids crying for their lost siblings, friends, and teachers. I had practiced intruder drills with the three- and four-year-old students in my classroom, shutting them in cubbies and pleading with them to keep a "bubble in their mouths." And on more than one occasion, I'd received text alerts from my own children's school, telling me they were on total lockdown because of reports of an armed person in the area.

It was scary.

It is scary.

According to MDA, every day one hundred people die by gun violence in America.[1] In the deep, dark, scary part of her soul, every mother I know continues to fear for her children's safety because our country continues to confuse commonsense gun reform with being against the Second Amendment. But I was going to change all that. I was going to go to a meeting! Armed with a fresh notebook and a *good* pen, I pressed on my HELLO, MY NAME IS: KELLY nametag and prepared to change the world. I felt noble, brave even, as the meeting's presenters fired up their PowerPoint presentation. While the women leading the meeting shared statistics and upcoming legislative happenings, I sharpened my active listening skills by nodding

1. "Everytown Responds to President Biden's Remarks on Tragic Mass Shooting in Boulder, Calls for Immediate Action," Moms Demand Action, March 23, 2021, https://momsdemandaction.org/everytown-responds-to-president-bidens-remarks-on-tragic-mass-shooting-in-boulder-calls-for-immediate-action/.

and furrowing my brow *really* thoughtfully. From the outside, it may have looked like all I was doing was creating a puddle of butt sweat on my metal folding chair in the back room of a public library, but inside, a powder keg was being lit. Soon I'd be sitting in on legislative sessions in our State house and handcuffing myself to NRA headquarters. What an incredible activist I was instantly becoming!

When the meeting wrapped, I headed to the back of the room where trifold posters with gun-violence statistics stood over sign-up sheets for various volunteer opportunities.

"Is this your first meeting?" an eager MDA greeter asked me.

"It is!" I answered triumphantly.

"Would you like to sign up for our email list or one of our volunteer opportunities?"

"I would like to sign up for all of them."

I grabbed the good pen from between the pages of my barely used notebook and wrote my email address on four or five different sheets of paper—with a flourish.

The very next day I got a call from the volunteer coordinator for one of the events I'd signed up for. Surprisingly, receiving that call felt significantly less exhilarating than putting my name on the sign-up sheet, a feeling I noted with some disappointment. The volunteer coordinator was reaching out because she needed a point of contact at my children's school to try and work with the administration to offer parents an MDA-sponsored information session. It wasn't the glitz-and-glam kind of assignment I'd been hoping for, but I agreed to the post and its requisite training sessions.

"I joined Moms Demand Action," I liked to brag to anyone who would listen, "and now I'm coordinating an event."

I was passionate about the information I was helping to spread; I believed it would change lives, and maybe even save some. I was also proud to be actively embodying something Brian and I had always wanted to instill in our kids, which was that if you see a problem, do something about it—even if it doesn't directly affect you. I didn't want to raise a family of ostriches, and being a point person for an event meant that I was leading my charges in the right direction.

In the weeks leading up to the MDA presentation I arranged at my children's school, I had to go to more trainings and make more phone calls. Timing had to be coordinated with the PTA, and the principal and vice principal had to be kept in the loop. And people! I needed to get butts in the tiny, tiny elementary school library seats.

It may not surprise you to learn that when you invite people to a "meeting in the library about gun safety," many of them will already have made plans for that particular Tuesday night at 7:00 p.m. And I don't begrudge them that. If they had invited me to a "meeting in the cafeteria to discuss proper handwashing," I probably would've had plans too. But nevertheless, I persisted. I posted about the presentation on social media and talked it up to friends. I reminded people who'd mentioned they *might* be able to make it and texted others who said to keep them in the loop. The day of the presentation, the volunteer coordinator and I chatted by phone about the pros and cons of having snacks (ultimately landing very much pro-snack) and figured we'd probably need enough goodies for twenty to twenty-five people—minimum. After we hung up, I worried that maybe I hadn't done quite enough face-to-face promotion or should've hit the Facebook contingent a bit harder. But that night when I got in my car to drive to the school, I assured myself that people would come.

And they did.

Two of them. Two people.

After all the preparations and planning and delusions of making a difference, exactly two women showed up to the presentation. And we had enough chips and cookies for forty. As I sat through the presentation that night, trying not to die of embarrassment and disappointment, I silently berated myself for doing a terrible job. And once I was done with that, I moved on to giving a mental tongue-lashing to all the people who didn't show up. *How dare they? Didn't they care? How could they not care about something as important as this?*

When the night eventually began to wind down and we half-handful of attendees started shuffling our handouts and putting water bottles into our purses, the woman who'd been presenting for us paused and said, "You know, I've been doing these presentations for a long time. Sometimes to big crowds and sometimes to small groups like this, and I always say that whoever was supposed to be in this room tonight to hear this message was here." Although I really believed in my heart that she was right, I also couldn't help but feel like she would've been righter if we'd had just a few more people.

I want to tell you that this discouraging experience only steeled my resolve to work harder. That I dug my heels in and fought for a cause that I believed in passionately. But I can't tell you that because my work with MDA fizzled after that night. As much as I supported their message, I felt too defeated to keep going. I blamed it on other things: a busy work schedule, our family expanding, and so forth. But the truth was, I was committing the cardinal sin of performative activism. When things got too hard, I gave up and moved on to save face. What I didn't realize was that in trying to curb any future disappointments I might experience with other poorly attended events, I actually made myself feel more ashamed over abandoning people who were working so diligently for this cause. It was a big, fat shame spiral, and I was just riding it all the way to the bottom.

Thunk.

When I used to run outside at recess, there was always that one kid who would quit the race before it was over. He'd blame it on an untied shoelace or a mystery muscle cramp, but the rest of us knew the truth. He was giving up so he didn't have to be the loser. And "technically" I guess this kid didn't ever actually lose, but he also never got to win. He never got to experience the sweet victory of crossing that finish line with his head held high, having given the race everything he had—even if he didn't come in first place. When I was racing on the playground, I was never that kid, but here I was a full-grown woman, giving up before the race was over.

Once I realized what I'd done in abandoning MDA after my extremely short tenure with them, I knew I needed to recalibrate. It had been so easy to get high on the idea of supporting an "it" cause that I hadn't thought to consider the possibility that my feelings weren't the most important part of the equation. That no matter how I felt on any given day, this cause would still need people to fight for it. I would actually need to show up and do the work, not just post the proverbial "black square" for clout. Not only for the sake of whatever cause I was supporting, but to teach my children that we don't abandon things just because they get hard. We stand with what we believe in and finish the damn race. Not so we can show off that we won, but so we can celebrate when everyone crosses the finish line together.

CHAPTER 28

Pandemicking

"This is all going to blow over," I texted to my best friend in mid-February 2020, while scrolling Amazon for surgical masks. "This is just people getting worked up over nothing" + *Liz Lemon rolling-eyes GIF* for emphasis.

I wasn't worried about the coronavirus,[1] I assured myself over and over. That kind of thing didn't happen *here.* In America. Where we had state-of-the-art medical care and top-tier healthcare professionals at our fingertips! And we had Purell. *So much* Purell. We'd made it through other scary-headline-producing disease outbreaks, and surely this would

1. Remember when we all still called it that? So formal. Now we're all on a first-name basis, like "F U COVID."

be no different. Germs like that couldn't survive here. We had tanks.

Still, I considered that it wouldn't be a terrible idea to take some basic precautions and stock up on a few emergency items, like bleach wipes and antibacterial soap. And masks. It wasn't like I was going to *need* them, but it might be a good idea to have a few hundred on hand—just in case.

I clicked the arrow at the bottom of the first Amazon page full of "unavailable" and "out-of-stock" masks, and then clicked it again. And then again. A tiny twinge of panic started to twist in my chest. Who knew there were so many kinds of masks? Were KN95s better than plain old N95s? What was a "filter insert"? And why did a pack of twenty-five paper masks cost $69.95? *And who the hell had already bought all the masks?!*

As news of what was happening in Wuhan, China trickled in over the course of the next couple of weeks, Brian and I would talk in whispers, out of earshot from our kids. "*Should* we be worried?" I asked, looking for reassurance, while knowing full well that we'd seen all the same infographics online. "Because this one chart that Kristen Bell shared looks like it's probably no big deal, but then *this* one that talks about some kind of 'flattened curve' makes me think we should be prepared for something kind of next level."

"Is this helpful for you? To keep talking about this when we really can't know anything yet?" Brian would ask, earnestly.

"*No*. Obviously, it's not. But they're closing the kids' school for 'deep cleaning' starting tomorrow, and I'm trying to get a handle on how much I need to spin out. Because if they're going to stay closed for more than a week, I don't know if I'm going to be able to handle it."

These were the kinds of things I would say at the beginning of the pandemic, before the actual gravity of the situation settled in. I could make bold (insensitive?) statements about "not being able to handle it!" and attempt to cope by stocking my pantry with three weeks' worth of nonperishable food items. Because what if the world really did shut down and I *didn't* have twelve cans of crushed tomatoes? *What then?*

It's a frightening thing, the prospect of being trapped at home. During a pandemic. Especially when you're a mom of young children. Not only are you trying to keep your family healthy and your home from imploding under the sheer weight of crusty dishes and only one functioning tablet charger,[2] but the pressure to not acutely mess your kids up during this defining moment in human history was intense. Because I must've missed the chapter in *What to Expect When You're Expecting* that covered answering questions like

Q: "Mom, when can I play with my friends again?"

A: "Oh, honey, I don't know."

Q: "Mom, when is quarantine gonna be over?"

---

2. Why is every charger in my house 8 percent charger and 92 percent frayed wires waiting to electrocute people? Is it so hard to make charging cables that don't disintegrate into thin air?

A: "Oh, honey, I don't know."

Q: "Mom, are you almost done crying?"

A: "Oh, honey, I don't know."

Like so many other parents, the weight of waking up every day and having to explain a crisis to my children in a non-scary way felt like a boulder on my chest. A boulder that was full of potential energy and then, maybe once it got rolling, eventually kinetic energy? Because on top of everything else, we also had to do science. And math. And reading, where I had to teach my kindergartener rules I didn't understand about long and short vowel sounds.

"Is *Schoolhouse Rock!* still an okay way to teach grammar?" I shouted to Brian one night from my typical school prep spot on the floor of our bedroom. "Or have they changed what we're doing with nouns since 1973?"

My notebooks, formerly used for my work prep and notes, were now filled with lesson plans and facts about the Revolutionary War that I'd googled in the hopes of masquerading as a competent teacher. And it wasn't just about teaching my kids the right information; it was about me wanting to give them concrete answers during a time when everything seemed so uncertain.

Like thousands of other families in America balancing school-age kids and working parents (thankfully, at this point Brian and I were both able to do our jobs from home), we were caught up in a fun and surprising turn of events: a dwindling toilet-paper supply.

"We are at 'DEFCON two-wipe max,' Bandas family!" I announced one morning after trifolding my rations of two squares of Charmin. The only female in a house full of boys, I was muttering to myself about the unfairness of human anatomy and their related toilet-tissue requirements when Archie's little face popped around the corner of my bathroom.

"Why did some people take all the toilet paper, Mom?"

"Oh, honey, I don't know," I half-sighed, half-answered, wishing for the millionth time that I had some incredible insight I could share with him about what the future would hold.

"I think maybe we could use leaves or—*gross!* Wouldn't it be sick if we had to use our old coloring pages?"

Yes, it would be, I agreed. It would be very sick. Although I did consider that it would be an effective way for me to dispose of the mountains of artwork I'd collected over the last decade. We *would* have to watch out for glitter—and our plumbing.

After that drive-by wiping conversation with Archie, I was struck by the fact that my children never seemed upset by the fact that I didn't have straight answers for all their questions—school-related or otherwise. They didn't seem panicked or afraid or any less reassured than they did when I would cobble together some answer for them about how gravity works or why Play-Doh dries out. They just accepted there are some things they can't know right now and then scampered off to fight over the good Wii controller.

I had convinced myself that my efforts to find answers for my children over the past few months had been for them, but in reality, I was doing it for me. To convince myself that I was in control and I knew best and I had got a handle on life. But as I watched my kids blindly put one foot in front of the other during one of the scariest times I can remember, I thought, *Maybe there's a better way.* Maybe accepting that I can't know everything all the time will actually set me free. And maybe that's kind of great. Because if I don't have to know everything all the time, that leaves a lot of space for me to grow.

~

We're slowly eking our way out of the pandemic right now, just as CJ is beginning to go through his "why" phase. I am very grateful for this timing, because I truly don't know what would have happened to my remaining neurons if we had gone through this stage while in lockdown. Although I will admit that this particular iteration of the "why" phase is extra adorable with CJ because he scrunches up his nose every time he asks it, and the little scrunches make his glasses lift up and down, making him look like a tiny, five-year-old Groucho Marx.

Like so many other kids, understanding the word *why* has opened up a new level of consciousness for him. He wants to know the why for everything.

Why did the milk spill?

Why is it time for bed?

Why is it too hot for his beloved Spider-Man sweatshirt?

And as much as I love answering his questions,[3] I am now learning to appreciate the times when I can't. Because I think it's important for him to know that Mom actually *doesn't* have all the answers. No one does.

We're all going through life wondering, just like him, one ply at a time.

3. *Most* of the time. Because who hasn't reached the point of "Good Lord in heaven, it's 5:45 a.m. I don't know *why* your sock feels like that!"

CHAPTER 29

The Coffee Shop

Lots of important things happen at coffee shops. Or at least that's what I tell myself as I lug my laptop computer from my perfectly good home office[1] to a wobbly table in the middle of a crowded restaurant filled with thirtysomethings discussing their Enneagram numbers while they sip on oat-milk lattes. I perch myself uncomfortably on a hard, wooden chair, my legs paradoxically both sticking and sliding in the early summer heat. It's uncomfortable and cramped, and yet I need this place. I need the clickity-clacks of keyboards echoing off the dings of phone notifications. I need the dull drones of Bible

1. A desk in my bedroom.

study groups *mmhmm*-ing and friends catching up in person after months of existing to each other only as blue text bubbles. There's something soothing about the soundtrack of a coffee shop, and so I show up in those spaces again and again, me and my laptop and *my* oat-milk latte.

As I sat on a Starbucks patio working one morning, a gentle breeze blowing and my leg skin poking through the holes in the seat like human bubble wrap,[2] I felt a general contentment about my place in the world. The sun was shining, but not in an aggressive way that made my computer screen impossible to read, and I was writing for a project I was really excited about. Most importantly, no one I knew personally had a cough that could potentially snowball into something much bigger and scarier. I was existing in that elusive place where nothing was really wrong *and* I wasn't worried about the infamous other shoe dropping, which, if you're an anxious person like me, is the Holy Grail of headspaces.

Generally speaking, if I'm not actively working on it in therapy, I don't get to live in that headspace very often. So as I was taking a moment to sit back and revel in a brief moment of caffeine-induced bliss, I noticed a Beautiful Woman sit down at a table near me. Her thick, wavy hair cascaded over her shoulders like an elegant, brown waterfall—which when I see it typed out doesn't create quite the word picture I was hoping for, but you catch my drift.

She was so beautiful that I was not the only one who

2. Honestly, who okayed this kind of chair design? All we want is a smooth surface to rest our butts on. Is that too much to ask?

noticed her presence on the patio. Every head of every iced-coffee-sipping patron in a ten-foot radius turned to stare as this woman sashayed by. If you can imagine Jessica Alba entering a scene in literally any nineties movie, it was like that.

Suddenly, I was acutely aware that I had not showered in, well, I couldn't exactly remember the last time, but my scraggly, messy bun suggested it was going on forty-eight-plus hours. Not that it *mattered,* because I was having an anxiety-free moment that I was not going to allow to be rocked by some personal insecurities about my looks. No way. Not me. I was s-e-c-u-r-e in my worth and value as a human person! So secure. Like, somebody give me a reflective vest and a Segway so I can work mall security, secure. I did not need to compare myself to anyone else, especially not anyone else sitting on this particular Starbucks patio with an insanely symmetrical face, and a great outfit, and a nicer computer than me. Because that, *that* would steal all my joy. And I was not about to let that happen.

And even though I was *not* going to let that happen due to my immense secureness, I happened to discover that if I angled my chair ever so slightly, the Beautiful Woman would no longer be in my eyeline, which was, like, totally not a big deal, but maybe also couldn't hurt. And so for a little while, I simply ignored her. Not on purpose, because I didn't *need* to ignore her, I just didn't want to actively be looking at her. There's a difference. And although you might think the contrary, I don't mean to suggest that I hated this Beautiful Woman. It wasn't her fault that she was making me feel inadequate. That part was very much on me, but it was just that her gorgeous presence was making me feel like a troll, and personally—*personally,* I found that annoying. Especially because I was under the impression that I was no longer being controlled by the opinions of others. Hadn't I abandoned that way of thinking? Surely my insecure, younger self wasn't resurfacing now to remind me that we'd never felt entirely secure in our body. That would be so rude of her.

Ruder still was the fact that after everyone else on the patio had gone and the two of us were the only ones left sipping our lattes, a couple of well-dressed, business-type folks walked up to the Beautiful Woman and complimented her on being beautiful and then asked her if she would like to be on a TV show. Now this type of conversation might strike you as Creepsville, USA, and give off major opening scene to *Law & Order: SVU* vibes, but as the only person sitting on that patio who wasn't handed an opportunity to appear on *E! News*, all I could think in that moment was

Why not me?

Why didn't those two well-dressed, business-y folks think I was as good as the Beautiful Woman? Why was she getting all the attention and I was being ignored, like some kind of invisible, irrelevant hag-o-rama?

But more importantly—why the eff did I care?

In that moment, my laptop fan kicked into high gear, signaling to me that it was either time to prepare for cross-check and takeoff, or to pack up and head home, so I stood up to gather my things. The robust "ouch!" escaping my lips as my legs painfully peeled from the seat of my metal chair was noticed by no one because, as I was fumbling to pack up, the Beautiful Woman was turning down the two well-dressed, business-y folks and getting back to whatever work had brought her to the coffee shop that day. Because, like me, she'd come there to disappear in the soundtrack of lips slurping and foot traffic melodiously parading by, not to accidentally set off a domino effect to expose all my personal flaws. And certainly not to be scrutinized by *me*.

Driving home after my brush with the Beautiful Woman, I considered that the obvious takeaway from the whole scenario was that I *shouldn't* think so much about what I thought other people were thinking about me. A sentiment that was both complicated grammatically and didn't matter. As a woman in her midthirties, I should scold myself for not loving myself enough to yell, "Screw all the haters," while I flipped the world the bird and did an ollie on my skateboard (because my cool alter ego definitely can ride a skateboard). And while it felt satisfying to bask in that mental loop for a minute, as I replayed the events of the day in my head, I realized I wanted to walk away from this coffee shop experience with an entirely different perspective.

Because no matter how much "work" I do on myself, how many books I read, how many ways I try to improve the way I see myself, it will never change the fact that I need to feel seen by other people. I don't think human beings are designed to walk through life without being validated in who we are. That's why we crave relationships and have a desire to connect with one another. Popular culture tells us that if we just do enough self-work, we can get to a place where we literally don't care what other people think, but that seems antithetical to what it means to be a person. We are designed to care about each other! And so instead of focusing on how we can block out other people's opinions so they don't change the way we see ourselves, I think we should instead focus on how we can make each other feel seen. How we can put in work to increasingly validate other people's experiences and hype each other up. Because it seems to me that doing that is a better use of our time than constantly telling ourselves the lie that other people's opinions don't matter.

Besides, other people are the reason I'm drawn to coffee shops to begin with. Their chatter, their clickity-clacking, their general just-being-there-ness. I do care about what they think and how they feel, and I want to be a part of their shared experience. As long as we all agree not to bring up each other's increasingly complicated drink orders. Some things are just too personal.

CHAPTER 30

In Defense of Real Housewives

I went for a run almost every single day from March 15, 2020, to September 15, 2020. Not because I'm some freak athlete or even because I was worried about gaining the "quarantine fifteen."[1] I went for a run every day during the darkest parts of the COVID-19 pandemic because I wanted to spend time with my best friends. I needed to spend time with them, really. Because you remember what it was like, cooped up in our

1. You guys, there was literally a killer virus spreading across the globe, and I sacrificed personal brain cells worrying about my jeans size. *Boooooo.*

houses for all those months, breathing in our family's stale, bad-breath air and having the same conversations on repeat all day long:

KIDS: "Can we watch TV?"
ME: "Later."
KIDS: "Can we have a snack?"
ME: "Later."
KIDS: "What time is it?"
ME: "Not later."

You and I know each other pretty well by this point, so I have to admit to you that my daily running excursions weren't always socially distant in the technical sense of the term. The honest truth is that when we met up every day, my best friends and I maintained close, personal contact the entire time we were together. And—*noneofuseverevenworeamask.*

I know! I know!

Now wait, before you get all retroactively mad at me for blatantly ignoring CDC guidelines, let me explain a little bit more about these friendships. The most important thing you need to know about this whole scenario is that my besties are totally blameless. I'm the one who *forced* them to come on runs with me; they had no choice. And truth be told, it's possible that they *were* wearing masks the whole time, because I couldn't see them.

Plot twist!

Now it's a perfectly acceptable thing for a child to have

imaginary friends. They give them adorably whimsical names like Mr. Boffo and Greg, but when a grown woman has an imaginary friend, people start to raise an eyebrow—maybe even two. But I am here today to end the stigma of adult imaginary friends, because I believe mine carried me through some of the darkest months in recent human history.

Now before this starts to take a real left turn, let me explain. My daily runs, while a little bit about exercise, were mostly about something else entirely. Because I saw the thirtyish minutes I spent plodding down the pavement in my neighborhood as a port in my pandemic storm. An oasis traveling at 6.2 miles per hour. It was my opportunity each day to be reminded that I was more than just a snack machine with two-day-old sweats on. I was still the same old me.

However, to maximize the potential of those thirty minutes, my tightly wound brain had to shut down every single last Lemony Snicket[2] of parenting-related anxiety. And the only way I knew how to do that was with my imaginary friends by my side or, more accurately, in my ear holes, chasing my cares away with talk of the latest *Real Housewives* drama.

If you haven't pieced it together already, the imaginary friends who carried me through the deepest parts of the pandemic were the podcast hosts I spent dozens and dozens of hours listening to during the time when I couldn't connect with my real, human-person friends face-to-face. And sure,

2. In my vernacular, a Lemony Snicket is a unit of measurement used to describe something very, very small, not a popular children's book author.

I realize this sounds Lemony Snicket[3] crazy, but instead of feeling embarrassed about this "hobby" of mine (aka being an adult woman who watches reality TV shows about other adult women solely so she can listen to her imaginary friends discuss them on a podcast), I am instead choosing to celebrate it—shout it from the rooftops, even. Because my genuine enjoyment of these podcasts highlights something much bigger and more important than just me getting my reality TV fix; it dignifies the idea that the things that help us feel content are never stupid.

I've spent many years of my life explaining away the things that help me feel like myself:

"I write this *little* blog."

"I just work *part-time.*"

"I make these *silly* videos."

And I think I do it so I can beat other people to the punch. It's my disclaimer that *I get* that the things I like are stupid. I'm in on the joke!

Oh no no no, I am aware that it's totally dorky I decided I wanted a neon bikini after I saw Heather Gay wear a neon bikini or that I could tell you exactly why Kyle and Lisa's friendship disintegrated during season nine of The Real Housewives of Beverly Hills. *I watch these shows i-ron-i-cally! I'm a valuable member of society with a well-calibrated internal barometer about which things in pop culture are acceptable for a woman*

3. Now that you know what this means, I can use it all the time!

my age to like. So please go on, tell me more about your intermittent fasting. . . .

Driving around my suburban town, I see this one bumper sticker all the time, usually on the back of minivans or SUVs or other kid-carrying mobiles:

I used to be cool.

At first, the sight of these stickers would give me a little chuckle. *I, too, used to be cool,* I would think as I shot a very hip thumbs-up to the driver. But the more I saw these bumper stickers popping up around me, the more I started to rage against them like *The Real Housewives of New Jersey*'s Teresa Giudice when anyone goes against *the family.* Because the truth is, you *didn't* used to be cool. You *are* cool. You are currently experiencing coolness. Just because you're not twenty-one anymore and you don't give a crap about the latest TikTok dance or Olivia Rodrigo single,[4] that doesn't mean you are a human joke who has to qualify her hobbies and interests with explanations and apologies. There is nothing wrong with leaning in to the person you are right now.

It's not always easy to embrace our own idiosyncrasies, especially when the world around us says we have to behave a certain way, but whenever I'm feeling shaky in the person I'm becoming, I'm reminded of a little piece of scripture from

4. Actually, I would consider caring about those because they are usually really good.

Luke, when Mary said to the angel Gabriel, "May everything you have said about me come true" (Luke 1:38, NLT). No disclaimers. No qualifiers. Not even a single hint of a qualm. On the precipice of becoming the *most unbelievable* version of herself that she's ever going to have to present to the world, Mary's all like, "Tight. Love that for me." And that combination of self-confidence and trust in God is where it's at. Not that I'm trying to equate my love for reality TV with Jesus' mom, but you get the idea. Be bold in who you are, and appreciate that there are some things in life that you love that you just can't explain.

I recently spent six months of my life going for runs with imaginary friends, and I don't for one second think that makes me any less valuable or relevant or cool than when I shopped for sparkly "going-out tops" in college. Because no matter what stage of life we're in, be it the Obsessed with OshKosh Overalls moment or Real Housewives Podcast phase, we have to give ourselves permission to do the things that make us feel like us, not just the version of us we want everyone else to see.

Because, to paraphrase the great Countess Luann from *The Real Housewives of New York City*, you are cool. You're not all—like, uncool.

CHAPTER 31

Balls

For Mother's Day this year, Brian bought me a subscription to a Plant of the Month club. Each month, a cardboard box containing a new pot, a dehydrated-soil brick, and a leafy green plant shows up on my doorstep, and I get the pleasure of unpacking and setting it up all by myself, just like a real gardener. Historically, I've not been great at keeping plants alive. One might say that I've had more than my fair share of failed window boxes and raised beds, but by some stroke of luck, I have managed to keep all my Mother's Day plants from going to that great, big garden in the sky—for now.

The most recent addition to my plant family was a batch

of three Marimo balls.[1] If you're not familiar, as I wasn't, Marimo means "seaweed" in Japanese. I learned, through the informational leaflet that comes with each of my plants, that Marimo balls are considered a national treasure in Japan and can live to be over a hundred years old. Of course, this piece of information immediately set my wheels spinning about who I'd bequeath my Marimo balls to in the event of my eventual demise.

Would the kids want to divide the balls or keep them together? Would Brian want ball-visitation rights? Would the balls ultimately cause a cataclysmic rift between my husband and sons from which there would be no return? WOULD THE BALLS RUIN MY FAMILY?

This is what I do to myself when I try to live my life from the future backward instead of from the past forward. I find myself getting very worked up over some balls that, according to the provided literature, should require "very little care." It's a good reminder to me to keep learning only from my past experiences and not my future projections, because if my past has taught me anything, it's that these supposedly low-maintenance seaweed balls will most likely be dead within a single calendar year, shriveled up like my poor guinea pig, Belle.

Our past experiences shape who we grow into, and because we just *keep* on having those experiences, logic tells us that

1. Listen, gang. I've learned that Marimo balls can have a highly invasive and dangerous species attached to them and therefore might not be a great addition to your plant collection. I'm not suggesting you go out and buy them; I'm just using them as a plucky little metaphor.

we should continually be growing throughout our lifetimes. *Much like the Marimo balls, which grow five millimeters per year for one hundred years!* Every piece of our story continually informs who we are becoming, which is hopefully someone who extends more and more compassion (to themself and others) each step of the way.

Back when we first met, I told you I believed that the world would be a much better place if people said things like "Good job" and "I'm sorry" to each other more. I still believe that, and so I want to leave you with this: Whatever you're carrying, whatever experiences you've been through, we've all made mistakes, but your story is valuable, you can keep evolving, and you are doing a really good job.

And also . . .

I'm sorry about all the times I just said *balls.*

Acknowledgments

First and foremost, I have to thank all of the Bandas Boys. Oliver, Archie, and CJ—you guys are the best part of every day, and I am so lucky I get to be your mom. Brian, you are an amazing partner and the greatest hype man I've ever known. Thank you for every time you said, "I'm impressed, but not surprised," and for all those nights when you reached over to rub my feet when you, too, were exhausted. I know we're not close to even in that department, and I love you extra for never reminding me of that.

To the Barons crew, thank you for being the most loving, encouraging, and funny family a girl could ask for. I'd choose you guys to be my family every single time. Also, I call the long couch.

A special thanks to my agent, Lisa Jackson, who took a chance on a rookie writer and helped me with every single step of this process. Without your belief in me, these words would never have happened, so thank you.

To my editor, Stephanie Newton, I'm so glad we found each other. Who knew that out of the mess of 2020, two Catholic, baseball fanatic, Outlander fans in Nashville would find a friendship? Thank you so much for going to bat for me and for all your guidance and thoughtful advice. I couldn't have done this without you.

To Jen McNeil and Lauren Bridges, thank you for your help in polishing and tightening up this project. Your insights helped me in ways you cannot imagine. Also, I am very sorry for my many, many spelling mistakes.

To the whole team at W Publishing, thank you for your continued support and your faith in me as a writer. It means the world.

About the Author

Kelly Bandas is a writer and comedian best known for her popular Instagram and TikTok videos satirizing everything from millennial motherhood to social media culture. Her work can be found literally anywhere you have an Internet signal (if your Internet isn't working, try turning off the Wi-Fi and then turning it back on again . . . or honestly, it could be your router). Whether she's hosting her not-at-all-dorky Outlander support group or speaking up about things that really matter, Kelly's mission is to always empower and lift up other women through community, inclusivity, and laughter.